How
NOT
to take it
PERSONALLY

10 Action Strategies
for Communications
Success in Business
and in Life

*To the five people who have been
instrumental in the shaping of my reality:
my mother Ruth, my grandmother Lily, my
best friend Gloria, my best coach Aneta,
and my dad Coloman.*

*And to the memory of my friend Dr. Niall
Morriss (Jan. 2, 1995) who in his final days
clutched my hand and smiled when I told
him of this book. Your courage inspired me.
I miss you.*

How Not To Take It Personally

This book is a value bonus. It contains many practical tools that the reader can exercise.

David Morrison, VP Training
Toronto Dominion Bank

Extremely interesting and excellent reading. There were moments when I couldn't put it down! The examples hit the nail on the head. I look forward to Ms. Held's next book.

Nancy Adamo, President
Hockley Valley Resort

Excellent insights and learnings on how to re-spirit and breathe new life into one's personal well-being and career.

Terry Mosey, VP Sales & Service (Ontario)
Bell Canada

Vera Held gives a fresh approach to identifying and working with individual communication styles. Her ideas are both informative and entertaining.

Betty Carr, Publisher
North York Mirror

A well thought out and practical guide to effectively interpreting and responding to the myriad of personalities we interact with on a daily basis.

Bonnie Bickel
President, B.B. Bargoons

How NOT to take it PERSONALLY

10 Action Strategies
for Communications
Success in Business
and in Life

VERA N. HELD, M.Ed.

McGraw-Hill Ryerson Limited

Toronto Montréal New York Auckland Bogotá Caracas Lisbon London Madrid
Mexico Milan New Delhi San Juan Singapore Sydney Tokyo

HOW NOT TO TAKE IT PERSONALLY: 10 Action Strategies for Communications Success in Business and in Life

3 4 5 6 7 8 9 0 TRI 4 3 2 1 0 9 8 7

Published by
McGraw-Hill Ryerson Limited
300 Water Street
Whitby, Ontario, L1N 9B6

Canadian Cataloguing in Publication Data

Held, Vera N.
    How not to take it personally

ISBN 0-07-552714-6

1. Interpersonal communication. 2. Communication –
Psychological aspects. I. Title.

BF637.C45H4 1996   153.6   C95-932382-1

Publisher: **JOAN HOMEWOOD**
Production Coordinator: **SHARON HUDSON**
Character & Inside Design: **DAVE HADER/STUDIO CONCEPTIONS**
Cover: **SAMANTHA TAYLOR**
Editorial Services: **DON LONEY/WORD GUILD**
Author Photo: **DAVID STREET**

Printed and bound in Canada

Contents

Foreword

Perspective! No matter what one tries to do, it's always lacking when we deal with issues or relationships that involve one's self. In this marvelous book, Vera Held sets out the tools necessary for one to gain perspective and, in doing so, learn how not to take it personally.

Every reader should find something of interest and utility in this book. We all get hurt and disappointed at times, and not always for the right reasons. Learning how not to take it personally starts with learning how to really hear what's being said, so the chapters on listening and language are vital. You might be able to see yourself in one of the 13 Potential Crash Sites in Chapter 2. You'll certainly begin to see yourself, your family members, your colleagues and co-workers in many of the different speaking styles discussed in Part II. Style differences, not substance, often lead us to, erroneously, take it personally.

Vera also understands that improving or developing yourself is not a passive activity. Real value lies in action, not simply comprehension. In Part III she sets out the ground rules on developing and implementing your own action plan for those who want to gain insight into finding a way to grow and improve.

The book concludes literally "on a high." Vera's got us in a helicopter surveying the vista, and learning to walk the human tightrope of life. We learn to make the necessary trades in life and in communication that keep us productive and keep us human. She also works hard to help us learn to nurture ourselves — something many of us forget to do in our hectic day-to-day lives.

Hats off to *How Not to Take It Personally,* a communications book that cuts through to the heart of why people get hurt and disappointed. A book designed to inspire, support, develop, grow and challenge you to be the best communicator you can be.

Michael E. Nairne
President, The Equion Group

Preface

*"In the middle of difficulty lies
opportunity."*

- Albert Einstein

My official, committed search for self-awareness began in January 1986. I was miserable, floundering in an unhappy marriage, and badly needed to understand myself, what I wanted and what I needed. So my first step was to find a coach to work with me. Actually, this was the same person I had worked with for a few months in September of 1984 but I had stopped because I was going nowhere. I was too scared then to do a reality check. I thought the status quo was the safest place to be. I was wrong. Things just got worse. So when I restarted in January 1986, I was prepared to get in touch with the real me — no matter what.

Things got much better, and at times worse, as I journeyed to understand how a smart person like me could have found herself in such a mess. The questions were tough, the answers even tougher, and making the changes inside myself were the toughest of all. I'd kept my real feelings bottled up inside for years until my whole body finally rebelled in January 1987 and said, "You're welcome to continue this nightmare, but I'm off-duty." And my body literally crashed with a number of stress-related afflictions. I realized how lucky I was that my body had been my guiding source, and I marvelled at how smart our human physiology is. I couldn't protect myself, so my body took the lead.

As there was nowhere to go but up, that's just what I did. I started taking care of myself intellectually, emotionally, physically and spiritually, got healthy again in each area, built a sturdy network of buddies, ended my marriage in May 1987, finished my master's degree in December 1987 and started my business full-time in

January 1989. I know this sounds succinct and perhaps simple, but in essence it was hard work, very inspiring, and took ongoing effort over a period of years.

Since then, my path has taken many different curves, but the self-awareness I gained at that critical time about my motivation and goals, my stressors, my body, my talents and skills, my desire to be an entrepreneur, my goal to thrive and not just to survive, my interest in helping others grow and my desire to coach became the foundation of the next nine years and for the life and business I have today.

My goal in sharing this journey with you is to emphasize just that. Self-awareness is a journey — and I made my mistakes and learned from them along the way. Some mistakes I even made repeatedly until I learned the lessons. Life has a way of making you repeat your errors until the lesson is finally learned.

Moving Forward

"The real voyage of discovery consists not in seeking new lands but in seeing with new eyes."

- Marcel Prévost

Through my own growth work and by watching and listening to others in business and in life, it became clear that there was a need to explore beyond the basic communication style mismatches. I saw people who were not happy. I worked with people who were not getting along with each other. People who were taking things personally and wasting their time and energy in the process. This also had a negative impact on the job. I understood and I wanted to help. So, I decided to investigate how and why:

1. Hurt and disappointment relate to our degree of self-awareness, self-knowledge, and to our perceptions and expectations of ourselves and of others.

2. A person's use of the features and tools of language in conjunction with their listening and speaking styles can create situations where hurt and disappointment can grow and fester.

3. People misinterpret and react personally to others' listening and speaking styles.

4. Those with challenging personalities (and there are so many of us) can be so easily misunderstood.

5. Our fears of people with challenging personalities prevent us from dealing with them productively and from really enjoying them.

6. Technology isn't always being used to enhance the humanity and clarity of our messages.

So, in December 1994, after sifting through all my data and getting in touch with my gut, I committed to writing *How Not To Take It Personally.*

My goal in writing this book is to help you become a communications success, both on and off the job, and to make your life the richest it can be.

Vera N. Held

Acknowledgements

To start, I'd like to thank my first communication teachers: my dad, Coloman Held, for always making language and culture fun, and for tolerating my many years of accent teasing; my mother, Ruth Held, for an early plunge into the world of adult poetry, which turned me on to the words (in my house you bypassed Humpty Dumpty and went straight to Robert Service); my grandmother, Lily Gurza, who was a funny and vivid raconteuse; and my wonderful primary school teachers at Briar Hill Public School in Toronto, who helped to knead and shape the dough.

Many high school teachers and professors along the way have also helped to influence my thinking and ignite my passion in my disciplines. A special thank-you to Eleanor Jungkind (English), Veronica Lacey (Spanish) and Brian MacDonald (Theatre) from Newtonbrook Secondary School; Dr. Roger Gannon (Sociolinguistics), Glendon College, York University; and Dr. Ronald Wardaugh (Linguistics), University of Toronto.

I'd also like to thank the following business associates and clients for their contributions: Marijane Terry of Geller, Shedletsky & Weiss Industrial Psychologists for helping in the design of the self-awareness and listening quizzes; Sue Carey from Lenscrafters for sharing her communications survey; Ross Tennant from Octel for simply being the voice-mail pro that he is; Greg Cochrane from Mariposa Communications Group for giving me the opportunity to work with his leadership team and to test-run some ideas; and a special thank-you to Michael Nairne from the Equion Group for giving me the opportunity to practise what I preach and for writing the foreword to this book. Throughout the book, I refer to numerous comic strips; I am grateful to the talent of these fine communicators in helping to illustrate my examples. I also want to thank the long list of clients, colleagues and business associates who made the time to speak with me, and whom I have quoted in this book.

To my talented group of eclectic friends, thanks for caring and sharing your best with me. To Gloria Estabrooks for juggling (in between flights and conferences) a critical read of my roughest of first drafts including valuable feedback, long-distance stylistic and spiritual hand-holding, and, very simply, for being a rock of strength and love in my life for the past 24 years. To Linda Maloney for Stormin' Norman, for her input on my short story *The Orange Cactus* where I first created "the Pricklies," and for always sharing hope, language witticisms and kindness. To Helene Pasen for her enthusiasm, insightful anecdotes and input on the challenging personalties chapter, acting as a sounding board often and well, for the phrase Crash Site Dummy, and for much appreciated and ongoing check-in calls to make sure this writer/rider wasn't feeling alone in the saddle.

To Karen Meyerowitz for her enthusiasm and support and her keen understanding of human nature on the challenging personalties chapter, for being an effective sounding board, and for "fun" hours spent on a much-appreciated critical read of my close-to-final draft. To Lisa Held for her encouraging and insightful letters all the way from Hong Kong. To Aneta Veisman, Leora Marcovitz, Bob Dameron, Wayne McCulloch, Chris Ballard and Robyn Wason who always made the time to talk about whatever was on my mind. (Over the years, they've often gotten an earful.)

This section wouldn't be complete without the long list of friends and well-wishers who were always a phone call and a word of encouragement away: Louise Wason, Sal Nensi, Mark Scarrow, Mona Younan, Jock MacDonald, Mick O'Meara, Dong Rosario, Wayne Sigen, Paul Litwack, Julie Michaels, Mary Anne Harnick and Jeremy Capel. And to the many, many others whose names I haven't mentioned, thank you.

Last, but not least, a heartfelt thanks to my publisher, McGraw-Hill Ryerson, and to vice-president Julia Woods and publisher Joan Homewood who put faith and dollars behind this first-time author. As well, I would like to thank the talented and enthusiastic team who all helped to make my book a reality: Sharon Hudson, Valerie

Bulanda, Sharon Budnick, Louise Abbott and Lynda Peckham-Walthert. A special thank-you to my publisher Joan Homewood for the intelligence, sensitivity and skill she brought to the text.

Introduction

You picked up this book because *"How Not To Take It Personally"* hit a nerve for you. So, let me ask you some questions: Have you ever been frozen to a halt by someone's comment? Have you ever mulled over something someone said to or about you 500 times trying to figure out how to interpret it? What it meant? Have you ever walked out of a business meeting where, no matter how well you negotiated, agreement was not reached and you took it personally?

Have you ever participated in "communication buildup," leading to what I refer to as the "10-year chronic grudge"? Dealt with people who won't forgive and can't forget? Have you ever been so hurt and disappointed by someone's action or comment that it affected many other parts of your life, perhaps for an extended period of time? If any of these scenarios are familiar, this book is for you.

How Not To Take It Personally is built on the premise that deep down, people want to communicate productively. To do that, sometimes we need to rethink or, better yet, reframe the way we think about things and hone our communication skills so that we listen "right," interpret "right," and respond "right." In the world of work especially, it's easy to take things personally that were never intended that way.

This book is about communicating options. About communicating health. About turning things around so the sky doesn't look like it's always falling. It's about responding — not reacting. It's about paving the road to self-commitment by becoming a first-rate thinker and a top-notch communicator.

Many of us spend our lives trying to get other people to trust us, believe in us, like us, understand us and, most importantly, accept us. First, our parents and siblings. Next, our teachers. Our peers. Our friends (actually the easiest group of all — endemic in the word friendship). Our mates, our employers and our co-workers.

1

As turn-of-the-century, high-tech eggheads, we also have to face an important fact: human nature has not changed. Our "egg-shell" heads are easy to peel, crack and break. Having once qualified as a total egghead, I know what it's like to take every comment made to me personally. Now, with many years of hard work, I take great satisfaction in having worked through the problem. I revel in all my new-found time and energy by (a) recognizing the person and the situation for what they are; (b) getting and giving clear messages based on both; and (c) successfully helping people and organizations grow and change through honing their thinking and communication skills. I still run into communication traffic jams, especially during the first snowfall of each year (don't you?), but now I enjoy the challenge of manoeuvring in and out of traffic, making mistakes and learning from them. And such is the path of continuous learning for the healthy communicator.

How Not To Take It Personally is a 10-strategy action plan to build your communications success in business and in life. This action plan will help you focus on the things that are important — you! You're important — your time, your energy, your productivity, your well-being.

This book is divided into four parts. In Part I, we will explore the basis of our self-awareness and self-knowledge: how to get it, how to listen to it and how to use it. Throughout the book, I use personal and professional anecdotes, and talking scenarios to illustrate how easy it is to ignore, get frustrated by or work with the cues inside you. How you listen to yourself leads to very different sets of communication results. So, becoming self-aware is an inward journey and the beginning to enhancing your listening, interpreting and responding skills. We then build on our self-knowledge and centre on identifying how and why other people can become hurt and disappointed. We identify 13 Potential Crash Sites and six techniques on how not to become a Crash Site Dummy.

In Part II, we look at listening, squash a bunch of listening myths as well as have some fun with the Six Listening Masks: the Daydreamer, the Attention Faker, the Distractor, the Self-Protector, the Selective and the Mindreader. We also delve into the dynamics of language and look at how, as different people, we use and interpret the Three Features of Language and the Three Tools of Talk in conversation. Combined with our six different speaking styles — the Lion, the Peacock, the Elephant, the Bull, the Chimpanzee and the Chameleon — it becomes clear how and why miscommunication is so rampant. By creating a Guide to your Listening and Speaking Styles, you can identify how style relates to getting your message across, and how these style differences or gaps can be misinterpreted and lead to hurt, disappointment and miscommunication.

After sharpening our knowledge and analytical skills in Part III, we practise 10 communication skill-building sets that include managing expectations, working with anger, being honest and letting go. We look at the Six Challenging Personalities that exist in the world today and create effective ways to deal with the Manipulators, the Experts, the Reactors, the Complainers, the Pleasers and the Pricklies to get the job done — while not taking it personally. We also look at using technology to enhance communication in relation to our three learning styles —our "but I want to talk to a real person" attitude — and the fact that we are still a society that's very "full of paper."

Last, in Part IV, we expand our self-awareness and self-knowledge. We talk about perspective and how to learn from our mistakes and implement our ongoing self-nurturing program to reinforce the successful communication habits we've built throughout the book.

Let me tell you up front that *How Not To Take It Personally* will move you 10 giant steps forward on the road to discovering how your expectations and perceptions of yourself, and of others, and of situations, impact on how you interpret and respond to messages.

This book will give you a solid basis for looking at yourself as a productive communicator in any circumstances — even difficult ones and with challenging personalities — because you'll be in control: of how you think, feel, interpret and communicate messages. Because, for the first time, you won't be taking things personally. You'll be responding — not reacting.

Face it — we can't change other people or shape their thinking or communication skills. But we are in control of building our own communication strengths. If we change the rules about how we listen to, interpret and respond to messages, we change our behaviour. At the same time, we automatically influence the communications behaviour of the other person. That's right! *Automatically.* And not only will we be able to take better care of ourselves, but we will be in a better position to take care of business too.

UNDERSTAND YOURSELF AND OTHERS BETTER

YOU ARE WHO YOU ARE

"Make It Thy Business to Know Thyself."

\- Miguel Cervantes, *Don Quixote*

Strategy 1: **Develop Your Self-Awareness and Self-Knowledge**

"Who are *you*?" said the Caterpillar.
"I hardly know, Sir, just at present — at least I know who I was when I got up this morning, but I think that I must have been changed several times since then."
"What do you mean by that?" said the Caterpillar sternly. "Explain yourself."
"I can't explain *myself*, I'm afraid, Sir," said Alice, "because I'm not myself, you see."
"I don't see," said the Caterpillar.
"I'm afraid I can't put it more clearly," Alice replied, very politely, "for I can't understand it myself ..."

\- Lewis Carroll, *Alice in Wonderland*

Like Alice, most of us don't really know who we are, or we think we know but aren't always sure. Most of us only know about half of who we really are — and it's impossible to grow in your listening, interpreting or speaking styles until you're in touch with the whole you, until you're truly self-aware. So, that's where we start — with you.

THE DANCE TRAP[1]

As children, we are trained like dancers to react to a piece of music and to move into the appropriate dance position. Our lives are choreographed in our homes early on. An eldest child might immediately protect younger siblings and take on the protector role for life. Or an empathetic youngster might always lend a supportive ear to a troubled parent and carry this over to other family members and friends. A child who is quick to make decisions may become a parent's confidante and continue in this role into his adult life. This is what I call "The Dance Trap". We become trapped in patterns that dictate our behaviour, patterns we're not necessarily comfortable with.

So what's the answer? First, we have to accept that how we listen, interpret and respond to messages is habitual. So, if you see some things about yourself that you'd like to change and improve upon, move forward but, at the same time, give yourself a break. It's going to be one day of practice at a time. Unlike Scrooge, who woke up from his pre-Christmas visitations a changed man, your growth will be gradual, so be patient.

In time, when you hear the old tunes playing, you will be able to respond with a newly choreographed dance — your dance, one that reflects who you really are today. The following story illustrates one of the learning experiences I had a couple of years ago that I used to break out of the dance trap and further increase my self-awareness and self-knowledge.

The Community Meeting

"If a house be divided against itself, that house cannot stand."

- St. Mark 3:25

I was invited to attend a community weekend gathering out in the country. As part of the retreat, an actual "community meeting" was held twice a day throughout the weekend. The purpose of the meeting was simply to share anything you wanted to share. I'd never done anything like that before with strangers. I was aware of feeling "new" and truly did not know what was intended or expected of the speakers or the listeners. Some people just vented their feelings. Others looked to problem solve. A couple of folks passed into sleep land. Others said nothing yet listened attentively. Everyone simply did his or her own thing and was accepted by the group.

As a coach, I was well experienced at working with groups and teams. But this was different: we had no specific goals, I wasn't leading the group (a shock to my system: you mean I could relax? and sit?), and it was my first time. I resolved to quietly participate and watch and listen. At times, I felt impatient, like I wanted to run out of there. I'm a private person, and this was just too much community for me. I wanted to skate or walk, have a good one-on-one chat with someone or play a good game of scrabble. But this action would not have been appropriate, so I stayed put and participated.

At one point, a vocal member of the group (and the friend who had invited me to attend the weekend) gave some advice to a man who had been describing how and why he'd been repeatedly disappointed by his employer. The man reacted negatively to my friend's advice, saying she'd "misunderstood and judged" him. The advice-giver, Vicky, then profusely apologized for hurting his feelings, burst into tears, and began to berate herself to the group for being insensitive and opinionated, and for saying too much at the wrong time.

At that moment, I reached out and put my hand on her shoulder and I told her she was being too hard on herself. Not only had her intentions been good, but her advice had been sound. Still Vicky refused to give herself a break for trying to help and blamed herself for making the other person feel badly. I realized how easily it could have been me in her place. Or any one of us. I give advice professionally, help if I can personally. And I, too, am not prone to giving myself too many breaks. I became frustrated with the whole situation and decided to say something. Now, two people were hurting instead of one and there could be more. I wanted to help if I could.

I told the group of this image issue I'd faced my whole life: strong people are able to give advice and take responsibility; they don't need help. Then, I asked them if they felt strong people ever needed support? If they had any idea how much responsibility strong people take for others' actions and feelings? The responses I got interested me:

1. Strong people never show their vulnerabilities.
2. Strong people don't need help — they're strong.
3. Strong people don't want anyone else's opinion.
4. Strong people like to be in control, and they make others uncomfortable.
5. Strong people are too demanding.
6. Strong people are intimidating.
7. Strong people build walls around themselves and never let you in.
8. Strong people like to be depended on.
9. Strong people like other strong people.
10. Strong people never act like they need anybody.

And the list went on.

I listened carefully to all of their responses, then told them that strong people need people and support too. That we're human, too. At the end of the meeting, several people rushed over to speak with me, to tell me my response was news to them, and that they would now look at strong people differently. A little more humanely, I hoped. I was satisfied that I had been able to plant a new seed with a few people. I also realized I wanted to do some more growth work in this area. *That I still wasn't 100 percent comfortable with being a strong person.*

Hot Water Bottle Syndrome

This situation helped me to rearticulate a familiar feeling, one that I'd been carrying around inside me my whole life. Being strong was a fact that I was proud of, but I'd always found painful. Part of me had always felt that being strong was some kind of crime. And for that crime, you had to stand trial — alone. You had to always do and say the right thing. You had to show integrity when others did not. You had to be fair when others were not. You had to be responsible when others were not. And you had to put other people's feelings above your own, because they weren't as strong as you. Being strong meant being a "Caretaker."

When I got old enough to label this ongoing phenomenon, I dubbed it the "Hot Water Bottle Syndrome." Initially as a daughter, as a high achiever in school and as a friend, I always thought it was my job to be the hot water in everyone's hot water bottle and to "fill them up," so to speak. I remember as a young teacher, leaving the classroom feeling disempowered, frustrated, disillusioned and plain depressed if everyone wasn't motivated or participating, or didn't excel and get what they wanted and needed — in spite of every effort that I could possibly have made. I remember many a time when I barely had the strength to drive my car home from school.

I began to ask myself some important questions related to being strong and being a caretaker: How could one person possibly be responsible to meet everyone's needs? Where did I stop? Where did they start? What was I responsible for contributing? What were they responsible for learning? How could I satisfy my competing needs for community and autonomy, power and solidarity?[2] I felt like I was in what anthropologist Gregory Bateson refers to as the "chronic double bind": if I gave too much, was I helping or hindering them? Was I helping or hindering myself? If I gave too little, was I unworthy of my profession? What was too much? What was too little? Do you give them fish, or show them how to fish?

I grappled inside with a constant push and pull to balance the sharing, the learning, the giving and the giving back, and simply taking. In time I gained perspective. In time I learned to walk "The Human Tightrope."[3]

I concluded that psychologist Carl Rogers had to be right when he said that a teacher is a facilitator who puts things down, shows people how exciting and wonderful they are, asks them to eat, then gives them the freedom to plan their own menu. And to catch their own fish! Anything else creates an unhealthy imbalance for both sides (and makes it damn difficult to drive the car home from school.)

On my ongoing journey to find balance in strength and sharing, I also revisited a comment a colleague had made to me a couple of years ago. "Vera, you don't need people," she critically stated when I told her I had travelled alone to South America for a month. I explained that my trip was full of people I met travelling and that I had sourced a list of contacts for each country I visited prior to going. I remember feeling uncomfortable by her comment.

How had she come to the conclusion that I didn't need or want to be with people because I'd travelled alone? I just didn't get it. What space, what rule, what perception was she coming from? Did she feel this was inappropriate for a woman to do solo? Did she herself lack the desire, skills and confidence to make such a trip, and was therefore taking a jab at me?

I asked her no questions, but I was left with an important question I needed to work through with myself: Why did I feel bad? The fact was, I travelled alone and it was a super experience. I'd done it several times before and after this trip. Her opinion was that I didn't need people, and she was welcome to her opinion. *But I let her opinion bother me.* Why?

What was clear was that I had always successfully done my own thing both personally and professionally. But along the way, I hadn't always taken full credit for my accomplishments and for who I was. I had taken her comment, personally, because my inner wall of self-trust was feeling a little wobbly.

So, what did I do? I took another look at me — the whole package. My communications image, my strong yet warm style, my need to initiate and to do things my way, and the possible ways different people could perceive me. Questions that helped me in my growth process around the issues of strength, independence, balance, listening and speaking styles and self-trust were:

1. What did strong mean? To me? To others?
2. Were strong and tough different? (I'd been called both, and tough was an adjective I then restricted to the plastic on car seats).
3. Where did my strength come from? How did I nurture it?
4. Was I "A Prickly?" (see Chapter 8).
5. Was it hard for me to show my vulnerabilities?
6. Why was being strong important to me?
7. How did I view people who were less strong?
8. Who were my friends? Why were they my friends? Were they strong? Stronger than me? How did we interact?
9. Did I need to become less strong to feel more accepted? Where did I need to get the acceptance from?
10. Did people find me challenging? helpful? motivating? intimidating? caring? sharing?
11. Was my image perceived differently by men and women? If so, by what kinds of women? What kinds of men? (professional? non-professional? younger? older? confident? not-so-confident? decision-makers?)
12. How did different cultures view my "strong personality"? (I'd travelled extensively, lived in Japan for a year, and had taught English as a Second Language for several years).
13. Where did my style fit best? In what kinds of organizations?

Like a Chameleon — Switch Gears

Over a period of time, working my way through these questions alone and with people I trusted, I came to a new level of self-knowledge and acceptance about my strong communications style and about myself.

Like the Chameleon whom we'll meet in Chapter 6, I was then able to switch gears to meet the needs of different kinds of audiences: to either put on or take off a listening mask; to slow down or speed up my speaking pace, moderate my body language, etc. to meet the needs of different kinds of people and to make them comfortable. I found I was able to continue to build an eclectic group of clients, colleagues and friends.

As my self-awareness and self-knowledge grew, I became more tolerant and flexible. I was able to recognize all the different kinds of communication skills that people would and could bring to the table. I understood what each party could give. What was possible.

In time, I became much less easily hurt and disappointed because I was clear about what I wanted and needed from other people and for myself, and what I could expect from certain people in certain situations. Where expectations could not be met, I revised mine after taking a discriminating view of my own expectations and what was possible, based on who the person was, the critical thinking and communication skills he possessed, and his level of self-awareness and self-knowledge. I no longer set myself up to be hurt and disappointed because of unrealistic expectations.

BUILDING YOUR OWN SELF-AWARENESS PROGRAM

So, you're asking yourself, that's how the process worked for her, but how can it work for me?

There are many steps in the journey to self-awareness, but most important is that you have a genuine desire to become self-aware and to continue to grow. Then, you need input from your own value system: your thoughts, your feelings, your gut. Next, you need input from others you respect and trust. Third, you need to pay attention to your behaviour in light of your new awareness: are you thinking about people and situations differently, and feeling differently? Are you communicating differently? And what are the results of these new behaviours?

To help you get started, here's a quick self-awareness quiz to get you thinking about some of your strengths and growth opportunities as we work through the book.

The Self-Awareness Quiz

What do you know about you? Please respond to the following statements with "always," "often," "sometimes" or "never."

Please circle your answers.

1. People are fun.
    always   often   ~~sometimes~~   never

2. I don't get hurt easily.
    always   often   sometimes   ~~never~~

3. I avoid interpersonal conflict.
    always   often   ~~sometimes~~   never

4. Miscommunication is inevitable.
    always   often   ~~sometimes~~   never

5. When a driver cuts me off, I take it personally.
    always   often   sometimes   ~~never~~

6. I am easily disappointed.
    always   often   ~~sometimes~~   never

7. Listening is hard.
    always   often   ~~sometimes~~   never

8. I learn something in every situation.
    always   ~~often~~   sometimes   never

9. I don't mind being wrong.
    always   often   ~~sometimes~~   never

10. I'm comfortable with myself.
    always   often   ~~sometimes~~   never

11. People who are more powerful than me, intimidate me.
    always   often   ~~sometimes~~   never

12. I try to understand people.
    always   ~~often~~   sometimes   never

13. In new situations, I adapt quickly.
    always   ~~often~~   sometimes   never

14. I like to finish what I start.
    ~~always~~   often   sometimes   never

Remember! There are no right or wrong answers. No scores or other people to measure yourself against. You're just finding out a little more about you, and what you're really like.

Now, what did you learn from the quiz? Did you learn anything about your strengths or growth opportunities? How optimistic you are? How confident you are? What's your desire to learn? Is conflict difficult for you? What kinds of people do you find intimidating?

Paint a picture of yourself — and take a realistic view. Which are the qualities that you consider assets and those that you believe are liabilities? Ask yourself what your strengths are and in which areas you feel you want to grow.

Remember! As in the case of my "strong" image, often a quality can have a double-edge, so ask yourself if there's something you like about yourself and at the same time want and need to increase your comfort level with.

Following is a sample strength and opportunity list constructed by an engineer named Bill. In a coaching session, working with a teammate he trusted, Bill developed the following list.

Things I like about myself and I am good at:
- logical
- good father
- careful with money
- treat people fairly
- good fisherman
- loyal
- work hard
- conservative
- team player
- good sense of humour
- tidy
- organized

Things I'd like to get better at:
- be more direct at work when there's a problem
- not get so disappointed when people don't come through on time for a project
- have more fun at work; I take it very seriously
- relax more
- schedule relaxation time with my wife
- feel more confident giving presentations
- trust my gut more
- make decisions more quickly

Bill has made a good start getting a clear picture of himself. He has many strengths and at the same time would like to improve at several things. So, how will Bill make decisions about what he wants to work on?

Course Correct Theory: Detect — then Correct

How do children learn to walk? First, they let caring moms and dads play backpack. Slowly, their little limbs and curious minds begin to develop and they want to crawl around on their own. Then what? Next thing you know they're hoisting themselves up along beds and tables, experimenting on all "twos." Then the exciting moment: they venture forth into unknown territories. They take a step. And boom! Fall flat on their behinds. After a mini-pout, they lift themselves up again, and try it again. This time they get in a step with each foot. Then lose their balance and boom, hit the floor!

But nothing deters them. They want to be on all "twos" like their siblings, mom and dad, people in shopping malls and the neat folks they watch on television. They learn something new from each effort, apply it and then try again until they're walking. They keep learning and keep applying — until they get it. "Theory in action" — that's how we learn.

Step 1: Detect

What are we detecting? Consider this quotation related to detecting when and why we are and are not listening, from Hugo Powell, chief operating officer — Americas, Labatt Brewing Company Ltd., "We need to realize that one reason people avoid listening is because it creates reasons to change. The corollary is true. If leaders bring listening and its newer truths to their organizations, it is more likely that people will confront reality and accept change. Good listening like optimism is a fundamental characteristic of successful innovators."

Questions to Ask Yourself:

➤ Do you listen to yourself and to others you trust?
➤ Do you avoid listening to your boss, your spouse or your colleague?
➤ Do you feel these people want you "to make a change" in some part of your behaviour and you don't want to?
➤ Are you aware of this behaviour? Do others point it out?
➤ Do you want to change? Are you happy with the status quo?
➤ Do you believe you can change?
➤ Do you believe you need to change?

➤ Have others specifically told you that you need to change?
➤ Were you able to "detect" the behaviour on your own?

Following are five strategies to get information and learn about yourself:

1. Tune into your thoughts and feelings.
2. Tape record your thoughts or write them in a journal.
3. Work with a friend or coach who can point things out to you that you might not be able to or don't want to see.
4. Read to increase your knowledge and then apply it to yourself.
5. Take notice and label your strong reactions to certain ideas, people and situations.

There is an old adage in Rules for Being Human (anon.) that says: "Others are merely mirrors of you. You cannot love or hate something about another person unless it reflects in you something you love or hate about yourself." So, when you have a strong reaction, monitor yourself. Ask yourself, what did that person trigger in me? Why do I like her sense of humour? Why do I like his way with words? Why don't I like how critical she is? Why don't I like how indecisive he is? To expand your self-awareness, you will most likely experience some uncomfortable and even painful feelings. This is a natural part of the process. Feel the feelings — *don't run from them*. This enhanced self-awareness will lead to increased options in how you look at and do everything.

Example: Detect the Interruption

Let's run through an example about noticing your behaviour that is critical to being a solid communicator. Let's say you have a tendency to frequently interrupt. You have slowly become aware of this, and both people you are close to and strangers have pointed this out to you (and haven't necessarily been pleasant about it).

It's important to note that in some situations, with some people (for example, your family, your work team), "talking over" each other is natural, appropriate and accepted by all, and there is no reason to look at modifying the behaviour. Our goal is to examine a situation where interrupting is not necessarily appreciated or accepted behaviour.

Questions to Ask Yourself:

➤ Why do I interrupt others?

➤ At what critical times in the conversation do I interrupt?

➤ Do I interrupt in particular kinds of conversations? (such as debates, negotiations, arguments, when I feel left out, when I feel I can't win, when I feel hurt, when I feel angry, when I feel intimidated, when I need attention, when I have something to add).

➤ How do I feel when I interrupt others? (in control? not in control? scared? not part of things? enthusiastic?)

➤ Am I more interested in getting attention than in giving it?

➤ Am I afraid of being left out of the conversation?

➤ Growing up, did I have to "cut in" to get my family's attention?

➤ How do others feel when I interrupt them? (anxious, hurt, offended, irritated, disappointed? that I'm too demanding? that I'm not interested in their opinion? that I'm assertive? that I have good ideas?)

Step 2: Weigh

Once all the data are in, you need to weigh the pros and the cons. Is it worth it for me to change this behaviour? You can do this in the form of an internal monologue, talking to yourself aloud (admit it — we all do this from time to time), dialoguing with a friend or writing it down. Following are some sample methods.

Questions to Ask Yourself:

➤ What are the advantages to changing?

➤ Is it less painful to change than to maintain the status quo? (Most people wait to make a change only when the pain in so great they have no choice.)

➤ What are all the benefits of changing? (list them)

➤ What are the trade-offs of the change? (list them)

Sample Benefit Paragraph

I want to be more likeable and to feel more a part of things. Interrupting is hard work and the results are negative, not positive. People don't like people who interrupt. They think it's rude. I succeed in pushing people away and this is the opposite of what I want. When I don't give them a chance to finish what they're saying, it stresses the relationship. Sometimes they think I don't care. I want to enjoy listening to others more and to feel less left out. I only can benefit in making this change.

Sample Point-form Benefit List
I will:

➤ connect with people in a more genuine and sincere way
➤ be better liked by people
➤ feel more a part of things
➤ work less hard to be liked
➤ learn to enjoy listening to others
➤ build my knowledge from listening to others
➤ be focused on the person and not the competition for attention.

Trade-Offs
I lose nothing in making this change and there is the potential to gain a lot.

Step 3: Decide

Make a decision to change/not to change a behaviour based on Step 2: for example, I will make a concerted effort to stop interrupting others.

Step 4: "Just Do It"

But remember, you will get better gradually. Don't expect overnight miracles. Use a martial arts approach: go with the flow of energy and be self-accepting.

Step 5: Make It a Habit

Reinforce the change all the time. As interrupting less frequently begins to pay off for you and your relationships, take credit for your work. Feel good about each successful interaction where you did not interrupt. Note the results, namely how you feel and how the other person feels, and re-commit to your decision to become a permanent non-interrupter.

LINKING MOTIVATION AND GOALS TO BEHAVIOUR AND CHANGE

What does it mean to be motivated to change? If motives govern our thinking and behaviour, why do we often fall short in meeting our goals? Let's say a person has decided that interrupting is impeding the building of a relationship, and he has decided to change this habit. He is motivated to do so and his goal is sincere, but for some reason he has not been able to change the behaviour. Why not? First, 95 percent of what we think, say and do is habit.

And second, as in my own experience as a teacher, we are not always able to easily balance our competing needs. As humans we all have a need to be liked and accepted and a need for community, which may require us to say and do things we are not always comfortable or happy with. As well, as humans we have a need to be independent, to have autonomy. But how can we be truly independent if we have to say and do certain things to be liked and accepted? This is the challenge of walking "the human tightrope" and keeping things in perspective.

Again, as normally functioning humans we must walk the human tightrope and trade things off one against the other. Our motives (like language, which we will delve into in Chapter 4) are dynamic and are in a constant state of flux. Caught in this chronic double bind, often our behaviour can appear confusing and contrary to others. So at times our own inner turmoil and behaviour can have a ripple effect; we can involuntarily cause other people to feel hurt and disappointed. Others can interpret words and actions personally that were never intended that way.

Growth Can Be Bittersweet

I'd like to end this chapter with a bittersweet anecdote about growth. As we have all experienced, sometimes when you grow and change, you can no longer meet the needs of a friend, colleague or partner. Following is an example of two friends who could no longer meet each others' needs and as a result their friendship dissolved.

EXAMPLE

Alexandra has moved into a "new phase" of her business. She has found that her time is at a premium as she is not only launching a new software product but she is also out of town regularly on business. To meet her schedule, she has told two good friends whom she was inclined to have "10-minute plus" conversations with during the day to contact her only after 5 p.m. Following is a conversation with Penelope (one of the friends) a couple of weeks after Alexandra established her "no day calls" policy.

Penelope (on voice mail at 11:00 a.m.): Hi Alex. I have a 60-second question about the GST. Would you please call me back?

Alexandra (on the run from a phone booth): Hi. I've just got a minute. (Penelope asks her question and she answers it.)

Penelope: I know you asked me to call in the evenings only, but that just doesn't work for me.

Alexandra: Well, days don't work for me, so how about weekends?

Penelope (tone drops): Okay.

Alexandra: Are you taking this personally?

Penelope: No, of course not. Speak with you soon.

Alexandra: Okay, I just wanted to be sure.

Penelope: Well, actually I wanted to tell you something about ...

Alexandra (firm): Let's talk on the weekend.

ANALYSIS

Alexandra has changed the rules of her friendship with Penelope. Penelope doesn't want things to change and has taken it personally. In Alexandra's mindset, Penelope is inconsiderate and has childishly retaliated; she couldn't talk to her during the day, so Penelope told her she couldn't talk to her at night. Alexandra's solution was to speak on weekends.

In suggesting the weekend solution, Alexandra dealt only with the facts and not with Penelope's feelings. Penelope was trying to tell Alexandra that she was hurt, but she didn't know how to. The bottom line: Alexandra was disappointed with Penelope's behaviour in not being considerate enough to accept her "policy," and Penelope was hurt because in her mindset this isn't how you treat a good friend. As well, Alexandra also felt pressured when Penelope wouldn't keep to the quick question-and-answer conversation. Although Alexandra was pressed for time, she still made the effort to return Penelope's call from a telephone booth as it sounded important. Penelope did not appreciate this and tried to keep Alexandra on the line.

Neither Alexandra nor Penelope called each other again. Six months passed and the two ran into each other at a seminar. The meeting was awkward and strained. Alexandra no longer cared enough to fix the problem and Penelope most likely was too hurt to say anything. The friendship was lost.

WRAP-UP

Sometimes when you grow, others can get left behind. However, if the friendship is strong, and two people make the effort, you will always find a way to sustain the friendship on some level.

Measuring Your Progress

How Not To Take It Personally is designed to increase your self-awareness and self-knowledge as it relates to how you listen, interpret and respond. Therefore it will be useful to identify:

➤ your current awareness of your communication skills that we will be working on throughout the book.

Remember! You are looking only at yourself and not comparing yourself to anyone else; and

➤ how often and deeply you become hurt and disappointed. Remember! As you learn strategies for how not to take things personally, both the frequency and depth of these "hurts" will decrease. Often we mask our hurts with anger. Be honest with yourself. Do you say you are angry or behave in an angry way, but inside what you are really feeling is hurt and disappointment?

The Communication Skills Awareness Quiz

Please circle your answers.

1. I set realistic expectations for myself.
   always   often   sometimes   rarely   never

2. I have realistic expectations of others.
   always   often   sometimes   rarely   never

3. My listening skills and habits are:
   excellent   very good   good   average   below average

4. Others think my listening skills and habits are:
   excellent   very good   good   average   below average

5. My interpretation skills and habits are:
   excellent   very good   good   average   below average

6. Others think my interpretation skills and habits are:
   excellent   very good   good   average   below average

7. My speaking skills and habits are:
   excellent   very good   good   average   below average

8. Others think my speaking skills and habits are:
   excellent   very good   good   average   below average

9. My all-round communication skills for dealing with challenging personalities are:
   excellent   very good   good   average   below average

10. Others think my all-round communication skills for dealing with challenging personalities are:
    excellent   very good   good   average   below average

11. My judgement skills for choosing the most appropriate medium (voice mail, fax, E-mail, etc.) for my message are:
    excellent   very good   good   average   below average

12. Others think my judgement skills for choosing the most appropriate medium (voice mail, fax, E-mail, etc.) for my message are:
    excellent   very good   good   average   below average

Carefully review your results and make some notes for yourself of the areas that you and others think you need to work on. For example, in number 11, if you circled "average," you might like to start thinking about ways to improve your judgement skills with specific media. We will talk about this at length in Chapter 9.

The Hurt Readiness Index

scale: 5 4 3 2 1 0

I would assess myself as:

5 – devastated by others' comments and actions
4 – frequently hurt and disappointed
3 – often hurt and disappointed
2 – sometimes hurt and disappointed
1 – rarely hurt and disappointed
0 – keep pin-pricks and bombs in perspective

It's natural to be hurt and disappointed at times. The goal of *How Not To Take It Personally* is to make sure that both the pin-pricks and the bombs are always kept in perspective. If you are sometimes hurt and disappointed, it would be helpful to make some notes as to the specific situations in which these feelings arise. If you circled 3 through 5, again make some notes for yourself. And don't worry — the strategies in the next nine chapters will help you gain perspective.

SELF-AWARENESS IS A JOURNEY

In a *Family Circus* comic by author Bil Keane, little Billy and his dad are discussing success. Billy envisages success as a long road filled with sweat and work hard. When he asks his dad if he'll ever be a success, his father reassures him he will, and reminds Billy that success is a journey rather than a destination. He encourages Billy to find a number of successes along the road. The last frame of the comic shows Billy happily zigzagging from side to side along the road of life enjoying a series of wins.

Whatever we find along our road needs to be met with acceptance. Longtime fears may come to light, resentments may surface that need to be dealt with, anger about a current issue, or the need for some support in a specific area. You might discover that you carry certain beliefs and feelings like "I'm a fighter" or "You can't trust anybody" or " It's a sign of weakness to ask for help" or "I'm not smart enough" or "He who rests, rusts" or "It's important to build on your strengths" or "I don't waste my time on losers." First, we need to accept these beliefs and feelings as alive and breathing. Once you've accepted your beliefs and feelings, you can choose to keep those that productively serve you. Equally, you can decide which ones you want to change or get rid of altogether.

And if you are really gung ho on your quest for self-knowledge, some big picture questions to ask yourself are:

➤ Why do you think the way you do? (about life, people, happiness, money, education?)

➤ Why do you behave the way you do? (are you easy going, demanding, critical, supportive?)

➤ Why do you believe what you believe in? (I must contribute to society; it's our responsibility to look after the elderly; I always tell the truth, etc.)

➤ Why do you value what you value? (family, friends, career, pets, material things, spiritual things, hobbies?)

➤ How have your communication skills developed? (family, teachers, boss, partner, children?)

➤ How did you develop your expectations of yourself and others? (family, friends, teachers, mentors?)

Throughout your journey, be fair to yourself and to others along the way. The often quoted Rules for Being Human offers some sage notions.

Rules for Being Human

1. You will receive a body. You may like it or hate it, but it will be yours for the entire period this time around.

2. You will learn lessons. You are enrolled in a full-time informal school called life. Each day in this school you will have the opportunity to learn lessons. You may like the lessons or think them irrelevant or stupid.

3. There are no mistakes, only lessons. Growth is a process of trial and error, a form of experimentation. The "failed" experiments are as much a part of the process as the experiments that ultimately "work."

4. A lesson is repeated until it is learned. A lesson will be presented to you in various forms until you have learned it. When you have learned it, you can go on to the next lesson.

5. Learning lessons does not end. There is no part of life that does not contain lessons. If you are alive, there are lessons to be learned.

6. "There" is no better than "here." When your "there" has become a "here," you will simply obtain another "there," which will, again, look better than "here."

7. Others are merely mirrors of you. You cannot love or hate something about another person unless it reflects in you something you love or hate about yourself.

8. What you make of your life is up to you. You have all the tools and resources you need. What you do with them is up to you — the choice is yours.

9. Your answers lie inside you. The answers to life's questions lie inside you. All you need to do is look, listen and trust.

Remember! We all have to follow our own yellow brick road to find the wizard inside of each of us. The journey to self-awareness and self-knowledge is ongoing: pleasant, bumpy, scary, happy, sad, angry, joyful and everything else in between. All the answers lie inside you.

To enrich your life, you need to expand your self-awareness, and to heed the advice of the smartest, diaper-bound philosopher I know — Trixie in Dik Browne's *Hi & Lois* comic strip. One New Year's eve, Trixie was contemplating her leap into the New Year. The sage advice she gave her readers was to take the New Year "one day at a time."

So Strategy 1 of the *How Not To Take It Personally Action Plan* is to build your self-awareness and self-knowledge.

Let's review the four steps to increase our knowledge and apply them.

1. Look, listen to and feel your feelings (even the uncomfortable ones) and monitor your reactions and responses.

2. Get input from others you respect.

3. Make a change in behaviour if it is good for you.

4. Continue to ask yourself questions; all the answers are inside you.

CHAPTER 2

PEOPLE GET HURT AND DISAPPOINTED

"People get hurt and disappointed because of unrealistic expectations. They perceive reality as they want it to be rather than how it really is."

- Michael Nairne, *President,*
The Equion Group

Strategy 2:   Develop Strategies on How Not to Become a Crash Site Dummy

In Chapter 1, we focused on increasing your self-awareness and self-knowledge, and I shared with you some of my own challenges, self-expectations and the expectations I found others had of "strong people." To look at options for productive communication, we need to explore how different people perceive the same situation — and the same person.

LIFE IS YOUR PERCEPTION, YOUR MINDSET

Antoine de St. Exupéry, author of *The Little Prince*, once said that "Words are the source of all misunderstandings." Equally, they can be the source of all understanding, revealing the mindset and perceptions individuals bring and share at the communications dinner table.

What are perceptions and mindsets based on?:

➤ our understanding and acceptance of ourselves
➤ our expectations
➤ our standards
➤ our life experience
➤ our knowledge
➤ our degree of optimism
➤ our education
➤ our language
➤ our culture

26

➤ our occupation   ➤ our level of accountability
➤ our position in an organization   ➤ our relationships with others

So, What Is Perception?

"The surest way to corrupt a youth is to instruct him to hold in higher esteem those who think alike than those who think differently."

- Friedrich Nietzsche

Your perception is your general outlook or perspective toward life and living, and there's simply no right or wrong when it comes to perception. How you see the world is just that — how *you* see the world. How "you" experience it and not your boss, your mother, your doctor, your next-door neighbour's cleaning lady, your son's principal, etc. Your perception is your reality. Equally, other people's perceptions shape their realities.

When someone talks about buying a new suit, for example, it may be from a second-hand store, from a catalogue, from a chain store or from a specialty shop. When a person talks of an expensive gift, is that a value of $20 or $100? Does a special dinner for four start at $25, $250 or $1000? When a co-worker talks about "the stress" involved in his new job, what does stress mean to him? And what does it mean to you? When an employee says she's been working "hard," what does that mean and how does it relate to performance?

In a *Mr. Boffo* comic, two hobos are sitting on a bench philosophizing. One tells the other that yesterday he was feeling like an "insignificant nothing" and today's he's feeling like a somebody because a fly just can't seem to get enough of him. This is his perception of what "important" feels like. In a *Larson* comic strip, one of two desperate men on a desert island will do anything to alter perception and have a little fun. While his friend is sleeping, he paints a pair of ships on his friend's glasses, then wakes him up pretending that he's spotted a ship. Perception can be influenced and changed, and is all relative to the person and to that person's situation. And to the quality of one's paintbrush.

So, What Is a Mindset?

"When we live up to the tapes in our heads, we are comfortable and secure. When others live up to our tapes, we are comfortable and secure around them. When they don't, we are uneasy and perhaps threatened. Others have similar discomforts about us when we violate their tapes or rules. When people's tapes are different, we have conflict or disagreement."

- Terry Mosey, *Vice President, Sales & Service/Ontario,*
Bell Canada

As Terry Mosey has reinforced in this quotation, we react to the tapes in our heads (The Dance Trap) and dance to the music we know and are comfortable with. Our minds have been choreographed to dance. Hubert St. Onge, vice president of Canadian Imperial Bank of Commerce (CIBC) Learning Organization and Leadership Development, defines mindset as the result of all of our experiences. "Our assumptions and beliefs form the lens of the eye with which we see the world and our environment. What can appear to be a pen to one person based on his mindset is a pointer for someone else. This in turn creates differences in how these two people will deal with the object and the situation, and will impact on their results. When we share and understand each other's mindsets and see the pen as both a pen and a pointer, we can work more effectively together and move situations and relationships forward."[4]

So, to understand someone's perception, to paraphrase Cicero, you need to "Think their thoughts, feel their feelings and know their words."

Organizations also have "collective mindsets," a set of assumptions and beliefs that are unwritten and appear to be invisible but are well embedded in the everyday culture of the organization. For example, a collective mindset in the banking world might be "never keep the customer waiting." A collective mindset in the service industry might be "always keep the customer happy."

Let's take this notion of imbedded mindset back to your organization. If you check in with your supervisor, is that viewed as respectful, considerate and showing commitment, or is it seen as being overly cautious, showing a lack of confidence, being needy? This identical action then could be perceived quite differently in different organizations.

Determining Fact from Opinion

"Anyone is always welcome to tell me I'm wrong. That's his or her opinion. But unless the person brings new facts to the table, my assessment of a situation or a person would remain the same. We would agree to disagree, and this wouldn't change our relationship, business or personal."

- Bob Dameron, *Vice President, Sales,*
Financial Services Industry

"There are no facts, only interpretations."

- Friedrich Nietzsche

In his quotation, a wise, adult Bob Dameron is able to clearly distinguish between fact and opinion. However, as children, some of us were not taught or couldn't recognize the difference between fact and opinion. I remember as a child certain people telling me I was "too smart," "too fat," "too poor," and that my hair was "too curly," my room "too dirty" and "too cluttered." What I didn't understand at the time was that these opinions were just that — opinions. Or interpretations, as Nietzsche puts it. Not things I should hurt over. These opinions had nothing to do with me as a person, and so in no way should have affected my self-image. But they did.

And how many of us as children interpreted other people's opinions as facts? And believed them, whether they were positive or negative? And how long did it take us to learn the truths about ourselves? Some people suffer from low self-esteem their whole lives by first believing others' negative opinions about them, and then by adopting those opinions as reality and living them. Others go the opposite route and adopt a perfectionist model, and find it very difficult to get along with and to accept others who can't meet their unrealistic standards. In either case, their self-perceptions can work against them and in the building of relationships.

EXAMPLE

Nicole, an architect, is speaking with her friend and business associate, Bernard, who is also an architect. Bernard is working on a new design project and Nicole is thinking of buying a house. Bernard and Nicole will team up for us from time to time throughout the book to illustrate certain speaking styles and strategies.

Following is their conversation.

Nicole (with interest): Maybe when your project is further along, I'll drop by for a look. I'm thinking of buying.

Bernard (indignant): These will be *first-class properties* and will sell for around $700,000.

Nicole (confident and deliberate): I am first class, but $700,000 is out of my price range.

Bernard (taken aback but listening attentively to Nicole's response, nods acknowledgement and utters a slow and deliberate "uh-huh" of agreement).

Nicole (smiles to give him credit for his response, quietly lets go a little sigh of relief and moves on to a new topic).

ANALYSIS

"Nothing gives one person so much advantage over another as to remain cool and unruffled under all circumstances."

- Thomas Jefferson

The important question is, did Bernard hurt Nicole? And the answer is an emphatic "NO." His comment, his opinion, his communication strategy, his style, his tone, his vocabulary choice, all of these things were about him. Bernard was communicating a social meaning about himself, not about Nicole, and Nicole in no way took his response personally. Rather she responded with a giant-sized dose of self-esteem, got great target practice, and had some fun.

This dialogue illustrates several things in relation to self-awareness. What did we see in Bernard's behaviour? Bernard's whole communications approach showed that he was not at all aware of the potential effects of his sarcasm, arrogance and snobbery. So much so, that when Nicole called him on his comment he was totally taken aback and had to reflect on it. He had no concept of how what he said could have been interpreted. Sociolinguist Deborah Tannen (1986) refers to two kinds of messages speakers give listeners. One is a content message and the other is a relationship message that gives you insight into attitudes, degrees of familiarity, levels of respect. Tannen feels we react most strongly to the relationship message. And she's right.[5]

The good news is, Bernard is smart and caring, and he was not out to intentionally hurt Nicole and she was confident of this. This fact was obvious in the time Bernard took to reflect on his comment and in the non-verbal feedback he gave Nicole. When he realized what he said could have been hurtful, he worked fast to correct it and the situation.

How would you describe Nicole's self-awareness? Nicole was able to respond quickly and expertly to Bernard's comment, and it is clear she has experienced this approach by Bernard and perhaps by others as well. Nicole is consciously competent; she knows her strengths and uses them. Her goal was to diffuse the situation as quickly and as painlessly as possible. She also wanted Bernard to learn something. Nicole focused on establishing a level playing field, one where money wasn't a measurement of character or self-worth. Once Bernard's power was diffused, solidarity was re-established on a human and intellectual footing.

Nicole is in touch with her need for balance and fairness and wants to be treated as an equal, dollars not withstanding.

She is aware that she needs to respond quickly and positively to counteract the potential effects of Bernard's bravado, for herself and for the productive continuance of the relationship. She is also aware that when dealing with the certain aspects of the Bull Style (more on this in Chapter 6) and in dealing with a challenging personality (Chapter 8) that she must remain calm and strong to have an impact. Meeting bravado with bravado would not have been productive (Bernard would just been goaded to fury). So, Nicole deliberately uses a calm, slower, intellectual strategy.

The Power of Expectations

Linda McCallister, in her wonderful book *"I Wish I'd Said That!"*, states that our communication success is directly tied to the expectations of the other person. Think about it — if you don't know how cold it is, you don't know how cold to be. I remember going dog-sledding in Northern Ontario several years ago, a day trip when the temperature was -40 degrees Celsius. Since then, my expectation of "cold" has been revised. Now even the coldest and longest of Toronto winters is much more palatable.

In dialogue, the same rules apply: when our expectations are met, we're naturally delighted, and when they are not met, it's easy to be hurt and disappointed. Or to be surprised and taken aback, like Bernard. If you don't have any expectations, or your expectations are conservatively low and are then surpassed, you're reeling from the bonus points. If your expectations are "too bright" or unrealistic, it's easy to fall short and perhaps disappoint yourself and others. In a *Farcus* comic, one of two gents shipwrecked but safe on an island, their ship sinking in the background, gleefully announces: "We could start by building a railway!" As you can appreciate, his unrealistic expectation wasn't met with a great deal of enthusiasm by his friend.

Because expectations are key to understanding how and why people become hurt and disappointed, I've created what I call the 13 Potential Crash Sites. Let's have a look at them.

THE 13 POTENTIAL CRASH SITES

When do we take things personally? When do we get hurt? Disappointed?

Crash Site 1

When we care about what the other person thinks of us and we want to live up to his or her expectations and standards, but can't or don't.

EXAMPLE

Anita, a freelance journalist, was working on an assignment for a client. She got pulled off partway through the project because of an internal situation at the client's. The client asked that she remit what she'd done to date with an invoice. Anita did, and the client balked at the fee. Anita demanded she be paid in full for the work she'd completed and, after 90 days, she was. However, Anita remained hurt by how she'd been treated, the fact that her reputation had taken a hit and that she most likely would not work with that organization again.

ANALYSIS

Could Anita have done anything differently? No. What happened here was strictly an internal complication in the organization and, as a by-product, Anita took a whack. Part of the reason she felt badly was because she was certain she was undeserving of the treatment. And other than fighting hard to get paid for her work, she had no control over the relationship with the client. It particularly distressed her that she was never told why she was cut out of the project. As well, Anita felt badly because the client will most likely not deal with her again, as it will bring up memories of the unpleasant strife in the organization. So even though Anita did good work, met deadlines and worked well with the client, the relationship was short term.

WRAP-UP

What can Anita do to get a handle on her hurt? She needs to walk the human tightrope and gain some perspective. She needs to take credit for everything she did right throughout the project.

a) Review all the facts of the situation.
b) Look at her product to take credit for its quality.

c) Accept the situation for what it is: an internal goof up.

d) Enjoy getting back to business.

Crash Site 2

When the other person's behaviour does not meet our expectations and standards, and we are disappointed.

EXAMPLE

Martha and Joel were going to a concert. They invited Cindy, Martha's friend to join them. They paid for her ticket and picked her up. Halfway through the concert, Cindy said she wasn't enjoying the concert and wanted to leave. Martha and Joel ignored her comment and all stayed for the balance of the concert. After they dropped Cindy off, Joel was angry and said he would never take her out again, while Martha was disappointed and hurt by Cindy's behaviour.

ANALYSIS

Martha's feelings of hurt and disappointment stemmed from several things. First, she and Joel had treated Cindy royally; she had been invited to the concert and her ticket paid for, and driven to the show. Second, Cindy had broken every etiquette rule in the book; she had been extremely selfish, insensitive and rude, and had shown no appreciation for how well she'd been treated. Had she expected that the moment she voiced that she wasn't enjoying the concert the three of them would make a beeline for the door? This hurt stayed with Martha for months.

WRAP-UP

Rather than ignore Cindy's comment, the conversation could have gone like this:

Cindy: You know, I'm really not enjoying the concert, and I'd like to leave.

Martha: I'm sorry you're not enjoying it. Why don't you grab a cab and we'll talk tomorrow? Joel and I want to stay.

Had Martha responded in a way to move the situation forward, and to be true to both herself and Joel, her hurt feelings would have subsided more quickly. That Cindy was not enjoying the concert wasn't her problem. After the incident, however, Martha may want to reflect on the friendship and what are realistic expectations of Cindy in the future. Do you think they'll ever go to a concert together again? Not in similar circumstances. What Martha has to be careful not to do though is to "throw the baby out with the bath water." I remember once an acquaintance went on a trip overseas to visit family he hadn't seen in many years. He returned home hurt and disappointed by the way he had been treated (I'm not clear on what his expectations were), and destroyed all the film from the trip.

Crash Site 3

When the other person shows us a new behaviour which is inconsistent to what we are used to, and we are surprised and disappointed.

EXAMPLE

Mary, an accounts payable clerk, has a work-related problem with her supervisor, Mark. Although they appear to have a good working relationship, Mary decides to take the problem to the manager without speaking to Mark first. Mark was irritated and disappointed.

ANALYSIS

Mark feels Mary should have come to him first to talk through any problem. This was the correct protocol to follow in his department and in the organization. As well, Mark is concerned about his image and how his superiors may view him. In the past, Mary had gone directly to Mark, but feeling dissatisfied with the results, she decided to go another route — over Mark's head. Mary did not intend to slight Mark; her goal was to fix the problem and to look after herself.

WRAP-UP

Mark is welcome to confront Mary on her protocol, but first needs to be prepared for an answer that he may not want to hear, and undertake a self-examination he may not want to perform.

Crash Site 4

When we are unable to accept that different people have different ways of showing how they share and care. These patterns could be quite different from our own; caring and sharing are inherently ambiguous.

EXAMPLE

In the fall, Ralph had moved into a larger apartment. His friend Bill had kindly lent him a rug for his living room as he didn't have one. As it grew closer to Christmas, Bill was wondering what to get his friend, so Bill asked Ralph if he liked the loaner rug. When Ralph responded with "yes," Bill bought him a similar one for Christmas. However, when Ralph opened the gift Christmas morning, he said out loud to visiting friends, "That's not a gift," and flung the rug to the other side of the room. Ralph was hurt and disappointed.

ANALYSIS

In Ralph's mindset, a gift means that you were thinking about him and got something for him with him in mind. He was disappointed because he felt the rug required "little thought about him," and was essentially a repeat of the loaner rug.

WRAP-UP

Lost in a self-absorbed mist, Ralph was unable to see how very thoughtful the gift was. Not only was there thought in the lending of the loaner rug, but there was both thought and effort in the purchase of a similar one.

An Expectation Met in Disguise

I remember the very first time I exchanged Christmas gifts with Gloria, my oldest friend. We were 14. Gloria disguised a lovely navy blue sweater in a bubble bath box. I still remember how horrified I was to think that she had bought me bubble bath. What a thoughtless gift! At least at 14 that was how I felt about bubble bath. Yuk! But Gloria was smart — and sneaky, too. She kept her cool as I very unenthusiastically opened the bubble bath box and out popped a great looking sweater.

Crash Site 5

When we want the other person to care about how we think and feel and the person doesn't, can't or won't.

EXAMPLE

For Christmas, Bernadette, manager of a mid-size investment firm, treated her staff of 20 to a buffet lunch. She picked up the tab personally, yet no one knew. With the exception of one person, who bought her a gift (which she feels was, for the most part, a political move), the staff did not acknowledge her thoughtfulness. Although she says she expected nothing, she was hurt and disappointed. She didn't even get a card. This has happened two years in a row.

ANALYSIS

No matter what effort Bernadette puts into a Christmas bash, it will not be appreciated. Bernadette is convinced that the people at this organization are simply "not those kind of folks." She nevertheless feels obligated to acknowledge the season, and in so doing, continues to hurt herself. She feels it's a no-win situation. What are Bernadette's options for next year's Christmas party?

– no party
– smaller-scale party
– pot luck and everyone brings a contribution
– ask head office to contribute
– suggest the staff go out and do something together (e.g., skating and hot chocolate, bowling, etc.).

But will shifting the task or the value of the contribution change how Bernadette feels? Bernadette feels obligated to do something, yet always feels disappointed afterwards. Do you think she'd be better off not to have a party?

WRAP-UP

Bernadette is a duty-bound type of person, and knows this about herself. She has clear lines and values on what she feels is right and wrong. As a result, she will arrange another party next year, regardless of how much it hurts her. For her, "doing the right thing" is more important than her own feelings. Bernadette often puts others' needs ahead of her own to walk the human tightrope.

Crash Site 6

When our self-image is a little wobbly, and we transform a pin-prick slight into a bomb.

EXAMPLE

Cathy visits Duke's home for the first time. They knew each other several years ago, and are now becoming reacquainted and have gone out a couple of times. Duke invites Cathy over for dinner. He lives in a fabulous old apartment building and Cathy is intrigued with the decor and fixtures. As soon as she gets there, she comments on the building's art deco decor and Duke's wonderful art deco light fixtures. When he shows her around the rest of his apartment, Cathy notices his closets. They remind her of her own: full. Cathy says jokingly:

Cathy: *Boy, have you got a lot of clothes!*

Duke: (quiet no comment).

They spend a pleasant evening together making dinner and enjoying Duke's piano.

Next day, Duke calls Cathy.

Duke: I just wanted to tell you that you intimidated me yesterday.

Cathy: If you feel intimidated, you are responsible for your feelings, Duke. I'm happy to talk about it.

Duke: That's true. I am responsible for how I feel. But you came in to my home, didn't say hello, didn't ask me how I was, and started making comments on everything. I didn't feel comfortable.

Cathy: I'm sorry I didn't follow all the rules. I was just excited about all the great old stuff in the building.

Their friendship continues. Then, a year and a half later, in conversation:

Cathy (laughing): You know, I haven't been back to your place for almost a year and a half. I remember you told me I intimidated you.

Duke: You made fun of my closets. That was personal.

Cathy: You were upset because I teased you *about your closets* and you're telling me a year and a half later? (Cathy bursts out laughing and Duke laughs, too.)

ANALYSIS

Cathy clearly did not follow "standard practice" when she visited Duke. As Cathy has realistic expectations of Duke now, she will make him more comfortable next time. Cathy might try slowing her pace, being less vocal in her observations and teasing only when she's certain that Duke is feeling comfortable.

WRAP-UP

How about Duke? What can he do differently? Now that he knows Cathy much better, he can be more objective about Cathy's behaviour. He also needs to take a good look at himself, and figure out why he reacted the way he did to this pin-prick. Although their communication styles are different, Duke is confident that Cathy was not trying to hurt him with her closet comment.

Crash Site 7

The false friendship: We trusted him as "a friend" and then found out that he or she was really a "business friend."

EXAMPLE

Pamela has set a rule in her department that if there is a problem, talk it through. She does not believe negative things should be put in writing as memos are permanent. Following is a situation with a staffer, Jeremy, with whom she felt she had a good personal and professional relationship.

Part 1

Pamela: Jeremy, may I speak with you for a moment?

Jeremy: Sure. What's up?

Pamela: The auditors need a signed agreement to change the payment structure for XYZ company. Do you have one?

Jeremy: Why didn't you tell me you needed one?

Pamela: The auditors found that XYZ changed their payment structure from $1,000 per month to $200 per month five months ago. You handle this account, and must have noticed the payment change, so we need to know if you have a signed agreement.

Part 2

Jeremy then wrote Pamela a letter (and you know how Pamela feels about letters), telling her she is making it impossible for him to do his job. Pamela first responded by phone, then in person. They finally reached a verbal agreement on how to handle the situation. Pamela asks Jeremy to initial and date his letter to her; however, he refuses, saying he never intended it "to go that far." Pamela was disappointed and hurt about the whole episode.

ANALYSIS

Pamela is amazed that Jeremy has been responsible for the account but for months has not noticed the change in payment structure. She expected more of him as this is his responsibility, his account. To complicate things, Jeremy asks her why she didn't tell him a signed agreement was needed. (Jeremy has been in this job for 20 years and this is the standard operating procedure.) Pamela is disappointed again in his lack of initiative and commitment. Then the major disappointment for Pamela comes with Jeremy's letter. Jeremy is feeling very threatened and very scared of potentially losing his job. He doesn't know how to handle the situation and chooses a letter as a form of protection in spite of Pamela's departmental policy.

Pamela takes the letter personally and is confused as to why Jeremy "did this to her." But in truth, Jeremy felt trapped and saw no other options. This is evident in his last behaviour — an inability to take responsibility for his actions and to initial and date his own letter.

WRAP-UP

Pamela handled herself professionally throughout the situation with the exception of one thing — she hurt herself and she kept hurting herself. She was unable to revise her expectations of Jeremy, and so she continued to let the situation and Jeremy disappoint her.

Crash Site 8

When we want and need something but don't know how to ask for it, and are disappointed the other person isn't giving it to us.

EXAMPLE

Carol and George distribute Bernie's novelty product and have been doing so successfully for many years. But this has never been acknowledged in any way. In addition to being Bernie's best client, Carol and her partner George have acted as consulting resources for Bernie on many occasions. Compensation has never been discussed, and they have given their time freely. George is hurt, disappointed and resentful. Both feel they have been taken for granted.

ANALYSIS

Carol has committed a total of 12 years to working with Bernie's product. She loves the product, has an ongoing and growing clientele who use the product, successfully sells it and makes a good income for herself and for Bernie. Yet she somehow feels taken for granted. Why has Bernie never taken her out for lunch? Bought her a gift? Lowered her distributor fees? Paid her for her consulting time to test new versions of the product? Does Bernie think her time is free? Does he take her for granted?

Bernie's attitude is that he is in total control as it is his product and that Carol and her partner are both dependent on him
for their livelihoods. Bernie feels he doesn't have to give or do
anything extra. That, quite simply, Carol and George should feel
lucky and grateful he and his product are around. And that, yes,
their time is gratis as ultimately they are helping themselves
whenever they or their clients improve on the product.

WRAP-UP

What practical options do Carol and George have in dealing
with Bernie? They can negotiate payment for their time in
advance and negotiate a break on the product price based on
volume. In both cases, they need to have very realistic expectations. Bernie views himself as in control and may not be prepared to negotiate on either point. At that point, Carol and
George would have to revise their expectations of working with
Bernie to make sure that in future they would not allow themselves to become disappointed.

Crash Site 9

When an emotional trigger goes off in us in reaction to a particular
action, word or idea, it can swirl us into an old pattern or The
Dance Trap. We don't respond in the present tense, the current situation.

EXAMPLE

Gary and Stan were going on a cruise together. Stan was carrying both sets of tickets and went to the counter to check them
both in. Gary insisted on having his own ticket and in checking
himself in. Stan was insulted and hurt.

ANALYSIS

Something set Stan off here. A trigger exploded and Gary got
knocked out of the ring. Although happy to be travelling with
Gary, a good friend, Stan needed to exert a kind of independence by checking himself in. Why? Had he had a previous travel experience where he didn't feel independent? Where his
actions were restricted? Did he feel a lack of independence in
other areas of his life? At work? With his family? With other
friends? Gary acted as if he were caught in an old pattern or The
Dance Trap.

WRAP-UP

Unless Gary confronts Stan, he will never know specifically why he reacted that way. Gary needs to weigh this decision in light of the whole friendship and how significant he feels this action was. What Gary must also do is not to take it personally: it clearly is Stan's problem.

Crash Site 10

When we project feelings of hurt we have with one person onto another.

EXAMPLE

Susan and Phil, two co-workers, are talking.

Susan (jokingly): Hey, Phil, how can you find anything on the desk? You're piled high with paper.

Phil (angrily): I know where everything is. You sound *just like my wife.*

Susan: Okay, okay, I was just joking around.

Phil: Sorry I snapped. It's been a bad day.

ANALYSIS

We've all been here. And if it's not paper, then it's something else. Phil likes paper and has a lot of it. And Marie back at the ranch has to put up with it and doesn't like it. At least not mounds of it. And she lets Phil know, too, and regularly.

Therefore, Phil doesn't take paper ribbing very well and snaps at Susan. This was further complicated by the fact that he was having a bad day. The good news is Phil owns up, and the potential hurt is quickly erased. It's amazing what an on-the-spot apology can do for a situation.

WRAP-UP

Can you relate to this crash site? I sure can. I'm a paper-plus fanatic: books, markers, envelopes, binders and more. Following is a conversation I had with a friend of mine when he came into my office a few months ago.

Joe (showing a wide-eyed look of surprise when he noticed my paper-full, art-full office).

Vera (smiling): It's a busy office.

Joe (diplomatically): Yes. (very thoughtfully and strategically) You have more paper; I have more computers.

As I know paper is an old trigger for me, I purposely addressed the issue up front. In doing so, I set myself up to respond productively rather than to react. And Joe, to make sure he wouldn't offend me, responded by drawing a comparison between his office and mine. He wanted to create a perspective by illustrating that different people value different things, and to make me feel comfortable. He did and is welcome anytime — as long as he doesn't notify the fire department!

Crash Site 11

"People get hurt and disappointed when they care. One reason this happens is when you don't accomplish what you set out to do and disappoint yourself."

- Karen Dobson, *Manager, Information Systems, Hitachi Construction Machinery Canada Ltd.*

EXAMPLE

Bill, a stockbroker, needs to fire his assistant because he is not capable of handling the job. Bill has been procrastinating about making the decision out of loyalty, a desire to secure a new job for his assistant with the company and to meet his own retraining and busy season needs. Bill is frustrated and disappointed.

ANALYSIS

Bill has not been able to make a decision on how to proceed and he's put himself into a box. His inability to effectively balance his competing needs has hindered his decision-making wrap-up. Bill is a caring employer; he is also a consummate professional and he is struggling with his priorities and his need to be fair to his staff. I should add that the staffer did a superb job in the first position he held with Bill, but couldn't make the leap to the upgraded position.

WRAP-UP

In talking through the situation with his coach, Bill concluded that he had to set a priority schedule for dealing with the situation: (a) he needed to secure a transfer position; (b) hire a new person earlier than he'd intended; and (c) commence training immediately to be ready for busy season.

Crash Site 12

When we wear one of our six listening masks (see Chapter 3) and we can't filter the information "right".

EXAMPLE

Pat has a busy job. His boss Irene offers him some help via a temporary staffer. Pat's reaction is a nasty, "I can do my job." Pat is angry and resentful at the offer and at his boss for making the offer. Irene is confused and disappointed.

ANALYSIS

Pat is wearing the Self-Protector listening mask and feels the need to protect himself and his territory. For some reason(s), he viewed this offer of help, which was legitimate and well intentioned, as a threat to himself and his job. Irene, although confused, accepted his response and posted the temporary staffer elsewhere.

WRAP-UP

Irene made a decision not to ask Pat to explain why he felt this way based on the fact that (a) it was inappropriate in an open office environment; (b) she felt you only get a certain number of chances with each person and she didn't want to use up one of these chances on this issue; and (c) she decided it wasn't worth her energy output based on previous experience with Pat. Ultimately, Irene felt sorry for Pat.

And now for the most challenging of the 13 Potential Crash Sites.

Crash Site 13

When we react (feelings) rather than respond (facts and feelings) but don't understand why.

EXAMPLE

Simon just put out his first CD. His cousin Richard told him he was "proud" of him. At the time, Simon responded with a shy smile, but he felt uncomfortable, hurt and angry.

ANALYSIS

Simon is the first person in his and Richard's family to ever produce a recording, and Richard clearly meant what he said — that indeed he was proud of Simon.

WRAP-UP

A self-aware Simon who wants to get in touch with his own feelings, goes through the following thinking wrap-up: "I'm certain Richard's intentions were nothing short of sincere. I could see clearly in his eyes that he really meant it and was giving me a compliment. But I had to stop and think about who in my life had told me they were proud of me. When, why, how often and what trade-offs (if any) were involved. Most importantly, who had the 'right' to make such a personal statement. Parents? Teachers? Close friends? Anyone? Everyone?"

In talking through the situation with his coach, Simon realized he'd put too much emphasis on Richard's "literal words" rather than his sincere behaviour. The words "proud of you" hit Simon's vulnerable spot, an old trigger. All his life, Simon had waited for his father to tell him he was proud of him, but the words were never spoken and Simon had always felt a sense of loss. He also had difficulty accepting this compliment from anyone else, including Richard, as it was his father's approval he still wanted.

Summary: The 13 Potential Crash Sites

In each example, analysis and wrap-up, we have seen how and why people could and would get hurt and disappointed, or how they could effectively reframe the situation to make it work for them. Whether it's because one of your triggers goes off, you've procrastinated and you're angry with yourself or you transform a pin-prick into a bomb, there's the opportunity to choose your response. Crash and burn, or reframe and respond?

The common ground in each of the potential crash sites is NO ONE CAN HURT YOU. You are in control of how you interpret the information and how you respond to it. *In fact, if you are hurt, you've decided to be hurt and have hurt yourself.* Equally, you have the ability to create the option to not get hurt. To reframe and to respond.

THE SIX TECHNIQUES ON HOW NOT TO BECOME A CRASH SITE DUMMY

I don't in any way want to sound cavalier in recommending that you simply decide not to get hurt. I know firsthand how difficult that is. And being human means being vulnerable. Some of our vulnerable spots are more visible than others (weight issues, nail biting, scars) and may be prone to comments. Other vulnerable spots are less visible (feeling successful, feeling fulfilled in an intimate relationship, having a solid sense of community) but are just as tender or more so.

You want to continue to show your vulnerabilities to the right people at the right time in the right amount — and to respond to any legitimate disappointments productively. Most importantly, if you are hurt, you don't want to stay hurt for too long because it's not good for you. Before we discuss The Six Techniques on How Not to Become a Crash Site Dummy, take a few minutes to re-read the headings for The 13 Potential Crash Sites. Which ones apply to you? What are your vulnerable spots? Make a list. This will be helpful in applying the techniques that will most benefit you to ward off any potential hurts.

Technique 1

In the age of "instant everything," don't feel compelled to respond in an instant. Once in a business meeting, a colleague demanded an immediate answer on something. My response was, "I'll have to think on it and get back to you by the end of the week." He wasn't pleased with my answer, but I was. How you defer in your answer shows your commitment and intelligence to reflect on what you will say. This reflection time and the quality of your response work together in creating your communications image and credibility, and are the basis of how you perceive yourself and how others perceive you.

Example

I remember giving a luncheon talk to a group of consumer affairs professionals. During the question-and-answer session, a participant said she had difficulty with customers who demanded immediate answers from her. All 35 participants readily agreed that they felt pressured to answer immediately. We discussed alternatives for responding to customers in a timely manner — minus the urgency. It's okay to jot down someone's name and number and arrange a convenient time to get back to them with the information. No one's house is on fire.

Remember! You are in 100 percent control of your response.

Technique 2

Ask questions. Many times people walk away from situations feeling uneasy, anxious, worried, disappointed and hurt because they didn't have enough information. When you don't understand why someone did or said something, or didn't do or say something, ask. You may not always get the response you would like, but this will allow you to clarify both the facts and your feelings and to diminish your hurt index.

Example

The seminar company Richard works with called to tell him that they'd received "a couple of letters of complaint about him" and that they wanted to talk to him about it. He was frustrated that he had to wait three days for an on-site meeting, angry that he wasn't given more information by phone and worried because he didn't have copies of the letters. Because he lacked information, his anxiety escalated to the point where he thought he was going to get fired. In the end, it was a simple content issue that was resolved in a half-hour meeting, and his job was never on the line.

Remember! You are in 100 percent control of getting the information you need.

Technique 3

Tell the other person how you feel and why, and try to talk it through. Perhaps he was just waiting for an opportunity to talk. Perhaps he will be totally defensive. But you won't know until you try. Take credit for your effort regardless of how the other person chooses to act. Make the first move and show your vulnerability and desire to fix the problem.

Example

I remember a conversation with a friend not too long ago. For several months, I'd been trying to fix a date with her to come over. For one reason or another, she never made it. I realized I still very much wanted her to come over, so I brought the topic up. She told me that I had made her feel guilty and that now she felt obligated to come over. My response was, "I'd love to have you over. My goal is to share some things with you." Her defensiveness immediately subsided and we picked a date.

Remember! You are in 100 percent control of your feelings not someone else's.

Technique 4

If someone purposely takes a jab at you, stand back — don't let the tip of the sword scratch you. It's not your issue. It's the jabber who's not a happy camper, not you.

Example

I remember telling a business friend that I was writing a book. Unhappy with his own work situation, his closing comment was, "Well, I hope I'll get a copy and that I won't have to buy it in the bookstore." My response was, "Well, I have some important steps to go through before I get to distribution, but I'll keep you posted."

Remember! It is 100 percent your decision to take or not take something personally — and to let it upset you. If it's not your issue, why get hives over it?

Technique 5

When something is important for you say so, clearly and caringly. Have you ever been in a situation where you are tied up at the office and a friend calls? What do you do? Don't be angry with the caller, but fix a time to talk that works for both of you. Make sure you deal with the facts and the feelings.

Example

Peter calls Melanie, his accountant and friend, to ask a business question and to see if she'd like to get together for a game of squash. Melanie is on a tight schedule, answers the business question and asks if they can talk about squash after five. Peter agrees and both get back to the business at hand.

Remember! You are 100 percent in control of stating what's important for you and of being respectful of others' feelings along the way.

Technique 6

If you feel a comment was intended to be personal, and it's worth it for you, question it.

Example 1

A few months ago I had dinner with one of my relatives, Sam. Two minutes into dinner, Sam says, "You know I'm angry at your mother. She never calls." (His wife had told me the same thing on the telephone the week before.) I responded to him the same way I had to her: "Why don't you call and tell her that? Maybe you'll find out why she's not calling you." Sam had taken my mother's not calling personally and was hurt, although he had no idea why she wasn't calling.

Analysis

Sam intended me to take his comment personally, in the hope that I would mediate between the two. I questioned the comment immediately as I felt it was important, did not take it personally, and put the ball back in his court — where it belonged.

States Betty Vernassal, a senior consultant with Forum Corp., "Occasionally comments are meant to be taken personally. Sometimes there's a chemistry mismatch, a power struggle, or you're just in the wrong place at the wrong time when someone needs to vent. To diffuse the emotion and remain objective, we need to focus on the potentially hurtful comment itself and question the person as to what was said and why. Generally, when people attack one another, it's out of fear or insecurity. For example, you might be doing something 'right,' and the other person might not be feeling that comfortable with himself and lash out at you."

Example 2

Marsha, a workshop facilitator who worked in the government sector, recently told me about three incidents all related to her nail-biting habit that demonstrate the various places and spaces people are coming from in the comments they intend to be personal but not necessarily offensive.

a) Marsha has just organized and run the first session of a workshop. She and a participant are talking. The participant turns to Marsha and says "You bite your nails." Marsha responds, "This is true" and unperturbed continues her conversation. Where was this participant coming from? Was she trying to find fault, an imperfection with Marsha? Was she feeling unsuccessful in comparing herself to Marsha and had to take a jab to make herself feel better? Was she just a jerk? As Marsha decided that the comment wasn't worth questioning, we will never be sure.

b) Marsha is at a trade show. She's meandering from booth to booth and stops at one. She introduces herself to Harry and they shake hands. As Marsha goes to pull her hand away, Harry grabs it back and says, "Hey, hey... what's this? You bite your nails!" As Marsha withdraws her hand, she says jokingly, "Yes, and it's my only bad habit." She quickly leaves the booth. What productive purpose was there in Harry pointing out her nail biting? Was he simply out of line? Was this his way of creating conversation, solidarity? Or, was he simply a jerk?

c) Marsha has been working off and on with Greg's executive assistant Trudy for about one year. Marsha has come to get some information from Trudy and has asked to borrow a pen. When Trudy lends her the pen, she remarks, "You bite your nails." Marsha says, "Yes I do." Then, based on the nature of their relationship, she asks Trudy why she made the comment. Trudy explains that she stopped biting her nails when she was 30 because, in her opinion, "it wasn't pretty." Marsha then confirms with Trudy that her comment was intended to encourage Marsha to give up the habit.

You Have Two Ears: One for Entry; One for Exit

As we saw, in the first two situations, Marsha chose to ignore the comment. In situation three, she decided to confront the person head on based on their working relationship and to secure a future one. How do you make these decisions? Consider the following factors:

➤ You know the person well and are certain that he or she is trying to be helpful not hurtful, so you decide to let the comment go in light of the "total relationship."

➤ This person "talks first then thinks," and is prone to making comments which you feel are better off ignored (you don't want to reinforce a negative behaviour by drawing attention to it).

➤ You clearly see that the issue mentioned belongs to the other person not to you, and you don't feel it would be productive to point this out to him.

Remember! If you want people to habitually demonstrate a specific attitude, action or behaviour you can choose to:

a) reinforce their positive attitude, action or behaviour:

Example

Gary enjoys it very much when Marge says "good morning" to him and asks him how things are going. To reinforce this behaviour, he gives her positive feedback (responds in kind, smiles, is pleasant, gives her a compliment if appropriate, etc.)

b) ignore their negative attitude, action or behaviour as Marsha did in the first two examples:

Example

Sally is a vice president in the Information Technology department. Greg, a junior, has forgotten his password. Sally teases him, saying "Hey, forgot your password again, eh?" Greg doesn't think this is funny, but decides it's not worth saying anything as she is his boss and he did forget his password — again.

c) confront their negative attitude, action or behaviour as Marsha did in the last situation:

Example

Sally has picked on Greg too many times now and Greg is angry. He tells Sally he doesn't appreciate the ribbing and that he'd appreciate it if she would stop. To stop Sally's behaviour, Greg's confrontation needs to:

- focus on Sally's behaviour and not her as a person
- be specific
- be short
- be forgotten and never mentioned again.

Remember! Perfection is impossible. Says Bonnie Bickel, the president of B.B. Bargoons, "I eliminate a lot of hurt and disappointment now because I don't look for perfection. I realized I'm not that perfect either." Set realistic expectations and be prepared to revise them as you go along.

So Strategy 2 of the *How Not To Take It Personally Action Plan* is to know The 13 Potential Crash Sites and The Six Techniques on How Not To Become a Crash Site Dummy.

Let's review the four steps to increase your knowledge and apply them.

1. Understand your own perception and mindsets for any given person and situation.
2. Identify what perceptions and mindsets others may bring to the table. Be prepared to stand (if not walk) in their shoes.
3. Know the difference between fact and opinion, and work appropriately with each in your decision-making process.
4. Become aware of your Potential Crash Sites, and design strategies for yourself to deal with each of these vulnerable spots.

Summary of Part I: Understand Yourself and Others Better

In Chapters 1 and 2 we looked at strategies to learn more about ourselves and others. In Part II we will apply this knowledge to Create a Guide to Your Listening and Speaking Styles.

CREATE A GUIDE TO YOUR LISTENING AND SPEAKING STYLES

CHAPTER 3

LISTENING IS COMPLEX, SO ...

"Listening, whether done by individuals or by companies and government, is a signal of respect. When people don't feel listened to, they don't feel respected. And when they don't feel respected, they feel anger or resentment. This resentment is exacerbated if people think you're pretending to listen but aren't."

- Hugo Powell,
*Chief Operating Officer—Americas,
Labatt Brewing Company Ltd.*

Strategy 3: Recognize and Interact Productively with the Six Listening Masks

SO, WHAT IS LISTENING?

Recently, while on break at a conference, I had the opportunity to eavesdrop on two managers. "My staff has so many poor communication habits," said one. "I know what you mean," said the other, "everyone talks, and no one listens."

How much of your time on the job do you spend listening? How much time do people spend listening to you? It's not hard to believe that up to 70 percent of workplace errors happen as a result of communication breakdowns.[6] And many are directly related to listening. Do the following examples sound familiar?

1. Ryan had the floor for 20 minutes at a team meeting; out of six people, only two had an opportunity to speak. There were mixed feelings about the meeting. Some people were frustrat-

ed. Others anxious. Some said they didn't care that they didn't have a chance to talk, but secretly some were fuming inside.

2. Jane wasn't invited to an important session she believed she should have been a part of. She was disappointed that no one had thought to include her, that no one wanted to listen to her opinion.

3. Henry and Paul, two continuous improvement managers, can't agree on anything — content, process, the weather — nothing. They are forever angry and snapping at each other and don't listen to a word the other has to say.

4. You ask one of your staff if something was done. You get a "yes," and later find out, based on the output, that the staffer didn't have a clue what to do, yet never asked for clarification.

As we saw in Chapter 2, our mindsets and perception impact our interpretation of each situation. Equally, how we see ourselves (Chapter 1), others and situations affects our attitude and our ability to listen and to interpret information. So, what do you really know about listening? Complete the true or false Listening Quiz on the next page to kick things off.

Keep your answers handy. Some of these are listening facts and some of these are listening myths which we will enjoy squashing in the next few pages.

SQUASHING THE LISTENING MYTHS

"Language exists only when it is listened to as well as spoken. The hearer is an indispensable partner."

- John Dewey

Have you ever heard someone's message but completely missed the point? Is what you think you heard what was really meant? Do you expect "intelligent" people (your doctor, lawyer, accountant, etc.) to automatically be good listeners? Are they?

The Listening Quiz

Please circle either "true" or "false" in the following statements.

1. Listening is an activity that comes naturally —
   everyone knows how to listen.

   True   False

2. People who are intelligent, listen better.

   True   False

3. Listening and hearing are different things.

   True   False

4. People who read a lot are good listeners.

   True   False

5. Good communicators listen more than they talk.

   True   False

6. The outcome of a conversation is controlled by
   the person who does most of the talking.

   True   False

7. Listening is important, but you can't easily use it
   to influence the thinking of others.

   True   False

8. What you hear is always what is said.

   True   False

9. Listening closely to someone means you agree
   with what the speaker is saying.

   True   False

10. Listening is an important skill in business and in
    your personal life.

    True   False

11. Training can help you to listen better.

    True   False

12. Listening involves more than the words that are
    spoken.

    True   False

Well, as you can see, listening is complex so let's have a look at the listening myths and see if we can squash them flat. When you are reading your way through the Listening Myths, answer the following questions honestly.

1. Which myths to date have I believed? (list myth numbers)
2. Which myths do I still believe in, even just a little? (list myth numbers)
3. Do you work with people who believe in the myths? If so, which ones? (list the names of key myth believers and the myth numbers that apply to them)

Myth 1: It's an activity that comes naturally — everyone knows how to listen.
False: Squash!

Unlike breathing, listening is a mental process. You must first make a decision to listen, then use your good listening habits to do so. It does not come naturally, it is not an automatic reflex, and certainly not everyone knows how to listen.

Myth 2: People who are intelligent, listen better.
False: Squash!

Have you ever tried to get your point across to someone you assumed was "intelligent"? A doctor? lawyer? your boss? And they completely missed the point? Have you walked away frustrated because no one tuned into your mindset? Well, listening has nothing to do with intelligence. Good listeners want to listen, and they make, and take, the time to do so.

Myth 3: Listening and hearing are different things.
True.

Yes, they are. Hearing acuity and good listening are not related. A person may hear well and also be a good listener. Equally, a person may hear well and not be such a good listener, or indeed may be a poor listener.

Myth 4: People who read a lot are good listeners.
False: Squash!

There are four communication skills. Two are receptive — reading and listening — and two are productive — speaking and writing. No communication skill is more important than another. We need to learn them all.

Because listening is a shared, social activity, and reading primarily a solo one, we listen three times more than we read. So listening can impact on our personal and business relationships and therefore our lives to a greater extent. People who read a lot in no way impact on their listening skills.

There is also an added health bonus to being a good listener. In J.J. Lynch's *The Language of the Heart* (1985), we see that people who are truly listening enjoy the benefits of a relaxed body, including a moderated heartbeat and reduced blood pressure.

Lynch notes, for example, that hypertensive people appear to be preoccupied thinking about what they want to say next almost as if they were continuously engaged in a contest or a fight rather than in a comfortable dialogue with the other person. Instead of listening, they appear to be defending against what others have to say.[7]

Myth 5: Good communicators listen more than they talk.
True.

Good communicators are concerned with understanding the mindset of the other person. What better way to find out about someone, than to listen to them? Good communicators ask questions, listen, watch, evaluate, ask more questions and keep learning.

Myth 6: The outcome of a conversation is controlled by the person who does most of the talking.
False: Squash!

Speakers and listeners are always equal participants be it a dialogue or a seminar where people are listening to a presenter or speaker. To give up our listening power, we are not being either fair to ourselves or to the speaker. A speaker draws his or her strength from an audience that is actively listening, and therefore actively participating.

Myth 7: Listening is important, but you can't easily use it to influence the thinking of others.
False: Squash!

Many people believe the stereotype that listeners are passive, not the actors, but working behind the set. Speakers must have active listeners or there is no sharing of a concept, a mindset, a thought, a philosophy. There is no opportunity to either persuade or to be persuaded unless true listening is occurring.

Myth 8: What you hear is always what is said.
False: Squash!

What you hear is your interpretation of the message, and what you understand is your interpretation of that message after you have filtered the message through your own potential crash sites. So, how much of the message is the other person and how much of the message is you? This is a really important question. Too often, people go with what they "thought they heard," with "I think he meant" or "I gathered from what he said that ..." when in fact they can't be 100 percent certain about what was message and what was their interpretation. It's times like this that a tape recorder can certainly come in handy.

Myth 9: Listening closely to someone means you agree with what the speaker is saying.
False: Squash!

When we listen, it does not mean we agree. Our process is to listen first. From there we decide what we need to draw a conclusion or to make a decision. More information? Time? Then we can agree or disagree or perhaps expand the situation, change topics. Options are endless.

Myth 10: Listening is an important skill in business or in your personal life.
True.

Poor listening can have serious short-term and long-term results. Good listening can save time, money and human relationships.

Myth 11: Training can help you to listen better.
True.

We hear people every day, but we need to train and build good listening habits. If we practice poor listening habits daily, they can become permanent. Most people listen at 25 percent efficiency.

Myth 12: Listening involves more than the words that are spoken.
True.

Listening takes into consideration the inherent skills of the listener. Our optimism, versatility, judgement, self-esteem, knowledge of what we are and aren't good at (conscious competence), our natural empathy, and our assertiveness. All of these factors taken together impact both our desire and ability to listen.

Understanding the Content Message and the Relationship Message

Listening also involves our ability to put together information from three areas: content, verbal and non-verbal. As the Mehrabian studies show, only 7 percent of a message is formed by the actual words we choose. Thirty-eight percent of the message comes from the verbal. By verbal, I mean the three features of language we will look at in Chapter 4: (1) intonation and pitch; (2) pacing and pausing; and (3) volume. Taken together, all three allow us to interpret things like agreement, discontent, sarcasm, hesitation, anger, pleasure, need for clarity, confusion, etc. Fifty-five percent of the message comes from the non-verbal: facial and body gestures, posture and eye contact. Edward Hall (1966) refers to paralanguage, or body language as we commonly call it, as the "hidden dimension" in communication. (We will discuss the added complications in written messages where verbal and non-verbal are absent in Chapter 9.)

Listening Beyond the Words

"When the eyes say one thing, and the tongue another, a practical man relies on the language of the first."

- Ralph Waldo Emerson

Example
Andrea and Colleen had an argument. Andrea called Colleen to apologize over coffee. After Andrea explained what had happened, Colleen said, "Is there anything else you want to share with me?" Although Colleen carefully chose the right words to encourage dialogue, Andrea carefully listened to her tone of voice, and was watching her facial expressions, her eyes, facial colour and body language. Andrea's overall reading was that Colleen wanted to avoid any further dialogue, so she responded, "Not at this time," and they moved onto other things.

THE SIX LISTENING MASKS

Now that we've squashed a bunch of myths that have created billion-dollar mayhem in business and in life, we need to address our listening masks. Like the actors of ancient Greece who provided their own masks fashioned of wood, leather or stiffened linen, we create our own listening masks for each occasion.

For the Greeks, the best masks were treasured not only because they were expensive but because through long use they had become extremely comfortable. Our masks, too, like comfy shoes or well-worn jeans have been with us a long time. Sometimes, we don't even know when we've got them on. As well, we keep our most treasured masks in excellent condition, in easy reach — just in case we need them.

For example, have you ever put on your daydreaming mask and caught a couple of zzzz's in a boring meeting? Have you ever nodded "uh huh" a couple of times just to get the person to finish what he was saying so you could get out of there? And when you felt the need to protect yourself, did you put on the Self-Protector listening mask? Let's have a look at our six listening masks, and determine whether we can see ourselves and the other people we work and live with.

Mask 1: The Daydreamer

Is basking on Cloud 9 and has unconsciously tuned out.

Mask 2: The Attention Faker

Faker A: Is dancing on automatic and has unconsciously faked his attention.
Faker B: Has made a conscious decision to fake his attention.

Mask 3: The Distractor

Distractor A: Is dancing on automatic and has unconsciously distracted himself and others.
Distractor B: Has made a conscious decision to either create or get caught up in the distractions.

Mask 4: The Self-Protector

Has made a conscious decision to protect himself by erecting a wall to shut the listener out.

Mask 5: The Selective

Has made a conscious decision to select the information he wants to listen to and ignore the rest for many reasons.

Mask 6: The Mindreader

Has made a conscious decision to mindread and not to ask questions for many reasons.

Remember! If you're the speaker, you have the opportunity to tune them onto what you're saying, thinking and feeling. If you're the listener, you have the option of taking your mask off if it is not moving the situation forward. But first, we need a couple of quick definitions to help us look at listening.

Monologue: One person talking at another who is not listening. Two people talking at each other, and neither is listening.

A "monologuer" will talk at people and not allow for any interruptions, or two monologuers will talk at each other at a cocktail party (for example, faking their attention). Monologuers are absorbed in making their point (or in being crushing bores) and are not interested in listening to your views. They are supreme Attention Fakers and can be a challenge to deal with.

Dialogue: Two or more people speaking and listening to each other.

In dialogue, on the other hand, both sides actively participate in speaking and listening, and trade off between the two activities as appropriate based on the nature of the relationship and the nature of the dialogue.[8]

Now, let's look at some techniques for dealing with The Six Listening Masks.

Mask 1: The Daydreamer

Ever been caught up in a pleasant daydream? Just taking a few minutes off to revitalize? Catching a couple zzzzz's? Caught up in your own thoughts — another assignment or meeting that you've been wrapped up in, that lingers with you, so you're really not "at" this meeting yet? Ever looked into someone's eyes and you just know they're in fog land?

Although we are able to listen and grasp up to 400 words per minute (people speak about 120 words per minute), the Daydreamer is on semi-permanent if not permanent Cloud 9 and virtually hears nothing and takes in nothing of what you're saying. The Daydreamer needs to be shocked to attention.

EXAMPLE

Cassia, a young copywriter, is doing a monologue in her head in a department meeting one Wednesday afternoon. She's been in non-stop meetings all day: "I can't wait until the weekend. I'm beat. That new movie *Thunderbugs* is going to start. Maybe

Jim and Nancy want to go Friday night. If I can get out of here before noon, I can catch them. The movie critic said ...”

Joe (noticing Cassia's inattention): Cassia, what are the two new ideas you'll be working with on the soft drink account?

Cassia: Pardon? (Cassia begins to defog when she hears her name.)

Joe (annoyed): Cassia have you heard anything we've been talking about?

Cassia (embarrassed): Well ...

Joe (persuasively): Well, this is your account, Cass, and it's a super opportunity to write some top-notch ads that will make the client happy, sell soft drinks, and put you in the winner's circle.

Cassia (committed): I've been working on a series of ads to come out monthly for the next six months. The theme is ...

ANALYSIS
When Joe catches Cassia in fogland, he brings her back to reality by first getting her attention and then by directly appealing to her need for credibility, accomplishment and for success. Cassia responds with enthusiasm and begins to share her campaign strategy and ad ideas. Joe got her attention and hooked her into the conversation easily.

How to Deal with the Daydreamer

If you're the speaker:
➤ get his or her attention
➤ be persuasive in getting them to participate (listening, interpreting, responding) by strategically pointing out the features and benefits to him of what is being discussed (WIIFM — what's in it for me, asks the listener)
➤ stay active and energetic (they're probably pooped).

If you're the Daydreamer:
➤ recognize that your listening mask is on:

In Chapters 1 and 2, we talked about self-awareness, self-knowledge and understanding other people's expectations. If you have your Daydreaming mask on, it means you are not aware that you have temporarily tuned out. To become self-aware is tough for the Daydreamer, because the Daydreamer is not at all conscious of his actions and therefore needs a wake-up call. For this reason, it is also the least potentially offensive of all the listening masks because the listener is truly unaware, and forgiveness will hopefully come easily from the speaker. We've all been in this position and can relate.

➤ take your listening mask off once you realize it is on.*

Self-awareness statements and questions like the following will help:

➤ "Am I missing something here?"

➤ "Oops. This is my project and I'd better get with it."

➤ "Boy, I'm tired. I think what Joe said went right over my head because my brain is still in the last meeting. I'd better stop him before he gets any further and ask him to fill me in on what I've missed."

➤ "I'd better swing into this meeting. Two meetings back to back gives you no breathing time. I don't want to nod off."

Follow-up Questions

1 What's one example of a meeting you partly daydreamed through? Who was the speaker? What was the topic? How were you feeling?

2. What's one example of a meeting where your boss or colleague was daydreaming? How did his or her behaviour make you feel? Did you do anything to snap him out of it?

3. Other than "annoyance" which we saw in our example, what other feelings might a daydreamer prompt from a speaker: empathy? anger? hurt? curiosity? disappointment? frustration?

Mask 2: The Attention Faker

There are two kinds of attention fakers: Faker A is on automatic, nodding his head and smiling in habitual mode, meeting after meeting. Faking has become a habit for him. He's honestly no more self-aware than the Daydreamer and could do with a gentle nudge to his nervous system. (Since we have already discussed the Daydreamer, we will not spend any time on Faker A). However,

---

* Note: Most Daydreamers are tired. If possible, be honest about how you're feeling and reschedule the meeting.

Faker B is a Daydreamer gone bad. He has decided to fake his attention because:

➤ it's politically correct to do so, or
➤ the discussion has little or no value for him, or
➤ he's heard it before but can't get out of the meeting, or
➤ he is preoccupied with other work.

EXAMPLE 1

Audrey has called a meeting for her customer service team. Alan, a customer service representative, is obliged to be there. He's really not interested. He has decided to leave the company as soon as he finds something else. He will participate only if called on (he's quietly hoping he won't be), and then he'll do the bare minimum to get by until he leaves the organization.

ANALYSIS

Alan's faked attention in the meeting is calculated. Based on the corporate culture, interactive departmental style and Alan's importance to the team, Audrey may be curious about Alan's behaviour and may have some questions for him. If you are faking your attention on purpose, always be prepared to be called on.

How to Deal with the Attention Faker

If you're the speaker:

➤ give the Attention Faker your attention (make him feel important)
➤ gain his commitment
➤ do regular security checks to see if he understood the points you made

Doing Security Checks

This can be in the form of questions, engaging the listener in a quick recap of the topic to determine what he understood, summarizing key points, asking for the listener's feedback, and constantly viewing and interpreting body language.

For example, I gave a talk for a charity grassroots group. I had no idea as to the group's backgrounds, interests or needs. So, I simply told them that and asked them to let me know what they needed as we went along. In the two-hour workshop, I did ongoing security checks to make sure we were on track and that they were getting what they needed. They felt comfortable contributing with questions and comments throughout.

If you're the Attention Faker:

➤ recognize that your listening mask is on. Questions to ask yourself:

- "Am I interested in what he has to say? I've got my friendly faker mask on. What does this mean?" (Remember! The key to taking your mask off is first being self-aware).

- "This might be important for the senior members of the team, but I don't understand what's in it for me. What do I get if I agree to go along with this plan? What are the features and benefits for me? I don't want to hear about it. It doesn't apply to me. I'll just sit here and nod my way through it."

- "I've heard all this before but I have to be here, so I'm going to fake it and think about something else."

- "I need to get back to that big pile of stuff on my desk. The ABC account needs ... The XYZ account needs ... This is not the right time for me to meet. I don't have the time."

➤ ask yourself if wearing the listening mask is moving the situation forward:

For Alan, the customer service representative, wearing his Faker mask is keeping him in neutral — exactly where he wants to be. He won't remove the listening mask unless he has to. Ralph the Attention Faker in the following example decides otherwise.

➤ take your listening mask off if it is not moving the situation forward.

EXAMPLE 2

Connie: Today's team meeting will revolve around the notion of leadership and communication. First, I'd like to get your feedback on ...

Ralph (monologue in his head, rolling his eyes and looking at his colleague Frank): Oh hell, here we go again. I really don't want to be here.

Connie (concerned): Ralph, is anything wrong?

Ralph (smiling): Everything's fine.

Connie: Folks, how would you like to proceed? Ralph, you're a pro in the leadership department — got any ideas for us?

Ralph (flattered): Well, I think a good place to start would be to get a definition of a leader.

Connie: Sounds good. I think I'll pass the reins to you.

ANALYSIS

Connie strategically gets and keeps Ralph's attention by gaining his respect and then by encouraging him to get actively involved. Many people attention fake because they feel left out and can't find value in the discussion. Participants who contribute can't and don't fake attention.

Follow-up Questions

➤ List one situation where you faked giving your attention.

➤ In a similar situation, today, how would you handle yourself?

➤ When you fake your attention, how do your feel? How could the speaker interpret this? (apathy? laziness? lack of commitment? preoccupied? other?)

Mask 3: The Distractor

Distractor A is a fidget widget on automatic. If there's something on the table to play with, he's got it. If there's a phone ringing, he's answering it. If there's music playing, he's tapping or humming to it or both. Added to this, he generally is trying to do three or more things simultaneously.

Distractor B is a fidget widget gone bad. I once tried to work with a person who talked to me, talked on the phone, sang, and did golf simulations all at the same time. Inevitably, when he got off the telephone, he needed either a washroom or juice break or both (no wonder) before our meeting could start — a consistent minimum of 15 minutes late.

EXAMPLE

Mary and Andrew have an important meeting scheduled for 10:00. Mary is at Andrew's office at 9:55. Andrew is rushing around, working on three things at once and tells Mary "he'll be a few minutes." Mary's time is tight and she is not pleased. At 10:15, Andrew asks Mary into his office, leaving the door open.

Mary: I'd appreciate it if you would shut the door. It's easier for me to concentrate.

Andrew (shuts the door): Okay.

Mary: And I'm on a deadline, so could you have your calls held during our meeting. (Mary's had this problem with Andrew before.)

(Andrew tells his secretary to hold all his calls except calls from two specific people and Mary starts the meeting.)

Mary: Here's the 20-page document I said I'd have ready for today's meeting. I want to ...

(There is a knock on the door and Andrew jumps up to open it. It's his partner, Dick. The guys kick around a couple of sports jokes, Andrew dashes out to get a juice, talks to a couple of people in the hall, then rejoins the meeting. Another five minutes have passed. Mary is frustrated and angry.)

Mary (angry): *As I was saying* ...

Andrew (jokingly while shaking his juice): Mary, you're so angry. Lighten up.

Mary (assertive): I'm angry for a good reason. You're not being respectful of my time, and I have some very specific goals to meet during this one-hour meeting. It's 10:20.

Andrew (quieter): Let's have a look. (Mary continues and things go smoothly.)

ANALYSIS

Although Andrew values his time, he does not value Mary's. He enjoys a variety of distractions and constantly creates them or interacts with them (in the hall). When Mary assertively lets him know how she is feeling, Andrew takes off his Distractor listening mask.

How to deal with the Distractor

If you're the speaker:

➤ let the distractor know what working environment you need to get the job done

➤ stick to the agenda regardless of any distractions

➤ stay focused on your goals.

If you're the Distractor:

➤ recognize that your listening mask is on:

- "Why have I got 15 things on the go here when I should be listening to ...? What's on my mind? Do I not want this meeting? I'm distracting myself, why?"

➤ ask yourself if wearing the listening mask is moving the situation forward:

- "Mary deserves my full attention. She's worked hard on her part of the project. Now it's my turn."*

➤ take your listening mask off if it is not moving the situation forward.

Follow-up Questions

➤ List things that you find distracting when you are trying to listen to someone.

➤ List things you do in meetings that others might find distracting.

➤ How many things can you pay attention to at the same time?

Mask 4: The Self-Protector

"Why does our supervisor always talk down to us? Who wants to listen to someone like that? I just turn off. At least I can get something accomplished when I'm in my head and nobody's making me feel lousy."

- Support staffer in a large Canadian corporation, in conversation with the author

The Self-Protector listening mask is evoked when its owner feels the need to protect. He or she erects a very cool 10-foot by 10-foot wall to keep all intruders out. They want to make sure they are not showing their vulnerabilities because they've put themselves in jeopardy before and are worried about being taken advantage of. People who put on this listening mask are particularly resistant to persuasion and to change. They find it too scary and keep intruders at bay.

---

* Note: If you are unable to give your full attention (for whatever reasons), reschedule the meeting to be fair to your partner and to the relationship.

EXAMPLE 1

Do you remember one situation where you felt the need to create emotional and physical distance to protect yourself? How did you feel? Let's have a look at Maryanne's situation.

Maryanne's boss just gave her a performance review: the worst she's had in 20 years of nursing. Her boss was abusive, gave opinions only and no facts. Her boss is "out of control," and upper management is looking into the situation. How did Maryanne handle it? She just listened but didn't get upset. She took nothing that was said personally but made mental and physical notes on the important points. She let the words pass over her like a warm breeze. Maryanne's response is atypical and healthy. By putting on her Self-Protector listening mask, she effectively protected herself from an abusive employer. Now, let's look at a more typical Self-Protector example.

EXAMPLE 2

Edward and Natalie have been working together a long time and are good friends. Both hard workers, Edward has just received a promotion. Natalie is delighted for Edward and at the same time she is hurt because she heard about the promotion on an E-mail announcement rather than from Edward. Natalie has avoided Edward for a couple of days. Edward knows why, and comes to her office.

Edward: Natalie, we really need to talk about this. I want to solve the problem before it gets any bigger.

Natalie (silent, arms folded).

Edward (softly): I'd like to fix this. I know we can. Will you give me an opportunity and just hear me out? I'd like to explain why I didn't come to tell you in person.

Natalie (a few seconds pass; Natalie unfolds her arms): Okay. I'm listening.

(Edward explains and everything is fine.)

ANALYSIS

Natalie has taken Edward's action, or lack of action, in the telling of the promotion, personally, and is hurt. Because she is feeling vulnerable, she puts up her wall to shut him out. Strategically, Edward appeals to her through warmth and gentleness, and slowly Natalie feels comfortable in letting down her wall, and in letting him in.

How to Deal with the Self-Protector

If you're the speaker:
➤ remember that behind the rigid wall is a warm-blooded mammal who responds well to warmth
➤ go slowly — this private property sign is humungous
➤ persevere — if it's worth it.

If you're the Self-Protector:
➤ recognize that your listening mask is on:
 - "I'm feeling uncomfortable and feel that I need to protect myself."
➤ ask yourself if wearing the listening mask is moving the situation forward:
 - "If I'm uncomfortable and on guard, Joe/Mary/Bernice must be sensing this too. Will this help or hinder the situation?"
➤ take your listening mask off if it is not moving the situation forward.

Follow-up Questions
➤ How do you feel when you've had to interact with someone who protects himself?
➤ What "warming up" techniques have worked for you in the past?
➤ Think of an example where you were the Self-Protector. How were you feeling?

Mask 5: The Selective

The Selective will pick up on a point(s) that is of interest to him and simply ignore the rest. In a Lynn Johnston *For Better or For Worse* comic strip, Elizabeth is playing with her baby sister April. Elizabeth points out to her mother that April is really beginning to talk: she says "gogg" for dog and "ba-ba" for bottle. The mother insists it's just all noise to her — until she says "ma-ma," that is. Then she immediately gets on the phone to give her friend Connie a full report.

Some consider salespeople who effectively do this to be real pros as they move the sale forward by selecting vital information from the client to work with. Equally, selective listeners opt out of dealing with information that leads to conflict, difficult decision making, painful feelings, embarrassment, etc. Let's look at the following example.

EXAMPLE

Patricia asked Ian, a pharmacist, to help her find a laxative product with cascara in it. The pharmacist said they carried no such product, and suggested several others to her with similar strength. Patricia thanked the pharmacist, then searched for the product on her own and found it. She returned to the pharmacy counter. This is their dialogue:

Patricia: Excuse me, but the product with cascara *is right here.*

Pharmacist: Oh, I thought you said you wanted something without cascara. (Gives an embarrassed smile.)

Patricia (Gives him a frustrated look and leaves.)

ANALYSIS

In a follow-up conversation with the owner of the drugstore, Patricia found out:

- They once had a laxative product called "Cascara" that had been discontinued.

- The pharmacist didn't know they now carried a product containing cascara.

- The pharmacist didn't know how to admit he'd made a mistake and apologize to Patricia when she returned to the counter with the product.

The owner was delighted Patricia had taken the time to call in and help him solve this problem with the pharmacist. He thanked her with a gift she chose on-site.

How to Deal with the Selective

If you're the speaker:
➤ make sure the selective hears what you want him to hear
➤ aim your rifle and keep shooting
➤ shoot until you score (or at least come close).

If you're the Selective:
➤ recognize that your listening mask is on:

- "Am I really listening to what she is saying? Am I only listening to what I want to listen to? Am I getting it?"

➤ ask yourself if wearing the listening mask is moving the situation forward:

- "She seems to be repeating herself and to be getting frustrated, so I'd better change my listening strategy. Something is not working very well."

➤ take your listening mask off if it is not moving the situation forward:

Follow-up Questions

➤ List one situation where you used selective listening and it furthered the meeting.

➤ List one situation where you used selective listening and it hindered the meeting.

➤ List one situation where the person you were dealing with "selectively" ignored something you said and it was important to you. How did you feel?

Mask 6: The Mindreader

Do you predict how the other person is going to finish his sentence? Often Mindreaders interrupt you and finish the thought on your behalf. The Mindreader works on the basis of making assumptions rather than asking questions, they tell rather than ask. This can occur for several reasons:

➤ you know the person well and are confident you know what he is thinking (and sometimes you do)

➤ you feel more comfortable working with your assumption because you might not like the other person's response (may lead to conflict, disappointment, change, fear, additional research and work, etc.)

➤ you're arrogant and assume "you must be right"

➤ you have to work with your assumption as there is no way to get any more information.

EXAMPLE

It's Wednesday afternoon and George and Gary meet by chance in the hall. Gary has been at outside appointments all morning and has just arrived at the office.

Gary (strategically): Hey, George, those Findlay papers were to be drawn up for Friday. Don't tell me — they're already done and they're on my desk.

George (carefully): Actually, they're in the works and they'll be ready for Friday at 2:00.

Gary (joking): Actually, I knew you were going to say that.

George (casually): I've got a question for you.

Gary (direct): Shoot.

George (good-naturedly): How do you always know what I'm going to say before I say it?

Gary (laughing and a little embarrassed): Just lucky I guess.

ANALYSIS

Gary is making assumptions about George's workload and priorities, and is checking to make sure Gary will be on time with the assignment. George is secure and non-defensive, knows George and that he is not trying to be hurtful in "checking up on him," and responds that way. George also assures Gary good naturedly that he doesn't need to play mindreader, and makes things easy for him the next time.

How to Deal with the Mindreader

If you're the speaker:

➤ let the Mindreader know that you'd like to finish your thought if they interrupt you or won't give you an opportunity to make your point

➤ correct the Mindreader's assumption in your explanation if it's incorrect

➤ walk the talk: make no assumptions, ask questions if you need more information and naturally act as a role model.

If you're the Mindreader:

➤ recognize that your listening mask is on:

- "I'm making a lot of assumptions about (things/situations/feelings) I can't be sure about. Maybe this is the way I want things to be but they really aren't that way. This could hurt the situation rather than help it."

➤ ask yourself if wearing the listening mask is moving the situation forward:

- "I need clarification by asking questions so we can proceed with knowing where we stand."
➤ take your listening mask off if it is not moving the situation forward.

Follow-up Questions

➤ List one situation where you interrupted the speaker and finished his or her thought and you were right.
➤ List one situation where you interrupted the speaker and finished his/her thought and you were wrong.
➤ How do you feel when someone interrupts you?
➤ Can assumption-making make for bad feelings? Think of something that has happened to you or someone you know.

Masks Are Fun on Halloween ...

The purpose of a mask is to hide your true visage, and that's exactly what our listening masks do. In Greek tragedy, to enter the playing area maskless was considered highly inappropriate. And even though comedians were allowed on stage maskless, their faces were always painted to obscure their real identity. However, unlike the Greek actors, before we decide to put on a mask in any communication interchange, we need to determine first if it will help our cause.

As we have seen, our listening masks can unwittingly push people away. But sometimes, as in Maryanne's case, "push away and protect" may be your goal. But generally we're in habitual habit mode; our civilization has a long history of the mask, and we don't even know we've got them on most of the time.

I remember once meeting an associate for breakfast. She talked, asked and answered questions but I couldn't feel who she was. What she valued. What she cared about. She wore the Self-Protector listening mask during the whole meeting. I lost all interest in getting to know her, yet that was the purpose of our meeting — and she was the one who contacted me.

The Listening Mask Spot Check

(Use this on yourself and others)

1.   Notice your comfort level with yourself (perspiration, how your gut feels, your ability to concentrate, your breathing).
2.   Notice your reactions. Are you focused on feelings?
3.   Notice your responses. Are you focused on facts and feelings?
4.   Are you being open and direct?
5.   Are you wearing a listening mask?
6.   If the answer is "yes," is wearing the listening mask moving the situation forward?
7.   If the answer is "no," take the listening mask off.
8.   Has a comfortable rapport been created between you and whomever else is involved?
9.   Does the other person(s) look comfortable (relaxed posture, willingness to both talk and listen, appear interested)?
10. Is the other person being open and direct?
11. Is the other person wearing a listening mask?

Remember! If you change how you listen, it will have to have an impact on how others listen too. As well, if you can peel off a listening mask and/or help someone to peel off his, it's just as refreshing as visiting your esthetician. And there are both short and long-term benefits.

So Strategy 3 of the *How Not To Take It Personally Action Plan* is to know the Listening Myths and learn to recognize the Six Listening Masks and how to deal with each one.

Let's review the four steps to increase our knowledge and apply them.

1.   Review the Listening Myths.
2.   Know the Six Listening Masks.
3.   Apply the appropriate strategy for dealing with each listening mask.
4.   Run the Listening Mask Spot Check to see if your mask is on and if it's serving you well. If not, take the listening mask off or try on another.

SPOKEN LANGUAGE IS DYNAMIC, SO ...

"When we study human language, we are approaching what some might call the 'human essence,' the distinctive qualities of mind that are, so far as we know, unique to man."

- Noam Chomsky, *Language and Mind*

Strategy 4: ***Know the Three Features of Spoken Language and the Three Tools of Talk***

Chapter 4 will deal with spoken language. We will link linguistics (how language works) with sociology and psychology to help us understand how people use language and respond to it in their day-to-day lives. (Written language will be addressed in Chapter 9.)

THE LANGUAGE FACTS

For linguist Michael Halliday (1985), spoken language is dynamic, that is, it shapes itself in the moment. Halliday too believes that in literate cultures like ours we tend not to take the spoken language seriously because it is so volatile. However, constant misunderstandings between people in business and in life demonstrate that we take all this "dynamism" rather seriously, and sometimes personally.[9]

Because of its dynamic nature spoken language, like creative energy, imposes a kind of volatility on the speaker and the listener. Being "in the moment" is hard work — making those on-the-spot word, grammar, pacing, pitch and intonation choices. As well, keeping human nature and the 13 Potential Crash Sites in mind, people can easily turn opinion into fact, misinterpret abruptness for

77

rudeness, and turn off or shut down to avoid listening when things are coming at them either too slowly — or too quickly. In a nutshell, it's easy to take things personally when "you're on."

Language Is Ambiguous and Relative

"Words must be taken to have one clear meaning."

- Aristotle, The Metaphysics, Book IV

Did Aristotle have realistic expectations about humans and about language? In light of all the variables we looked at in Chapter 2 that create and affect a person's perception, this seems like an impossible task. In Lewis Carroll's *Through the Looking Glass* (1872), Alice and Humpty Dumpty are arguing about this very same issue:

> "When I use a word," Humpty Dumpty said, in rather a scornful tone, "it means just what I choose it to mean — neither more nor less."
>
> "The question is," said Alice, "whether you can make words mean so many different things."
>
> "The question is," said Humpty Dumpty, "which is to be master — that's all."

Although our goal in speaking is a "precise mastery" of the words, as Aristotle and Humpty contend, as we know, human beings' individual perceptions allow them to interpret meaning. And that's a complex process. There are also inherent ambiguities in the English language itself ("the lamb is hot" has at least three meanings if not more in English) which can add to the fun. So deriving chunks of meaning from the actual words we choose is fun, often an adventure, and can be quite challenging based on all the possible interpretations.

And there's more. What is the relationship between language and thought? Much like language and culture, language and thought appear to be interdependent and intertwined. One key linguistic theory called "The Sapir-Whorf Hypothesis" says that many of our perceptions are structured through our native languages. We look at the kaleidoscope of information in the world and slice and dice it into chunks of meaning based on the pattern of our language. Every speaker sees the world through his native language; therefore, people from Italy, Germany, Israel, Papua New Guinea and Guatemala may have different world views.[10]

Language and Logic

"Two-thirds of the world is not the Western World. These people think differently .... Their words are not our words."

- Leo Buscaglia, *Living, Loving & Learning*

Equally important, people from different language and cultural groups use different logic patterns. Therefore, whether you are sending or receiving messages, you have to be prepared to adapt your thinking style. In Japan, I spent a lot of time waiting for answers. Why? The Japanese rhetoric or logic pattern is both circular and holistic: a Japanese speaker will begin at the end of an idea and carefully work back to the beginning when answering a question. In doing so, he or she gives the listener a full picture of the situation, but it does take time.

In the logic patterns of Latin-based or "romance" languages, all important elements are stressed, but not in the same order as in English. The logic pattern of a native English speaker looks linear but is actually circular and moves from A to B to C (with C, the end tying clearly back to A, the start.) A Francophone, on the other hand, may start with point A and then go to points D and C, ending with point B. As you can appreciate, a listener unprepared for the French speaker's logic pattern may get quite confused and miscommunication can easily take place.[11]

So, How Many Englishes Are There?

"The greatest barrier between the English and the Americans is that they speak the same language."

- Oscar Wilde, *Notes on a Tour of the United States* (1883)

English speakers around the world see the world through their own pair of English-language prescription lenses, and are in fact speaking different kinds of English. English has two geographic varieties: British English and North American English. There are several branches of British English — for example, Australian English and New Zealand English — and within these branches there are many regional and social dialects. North American English has two branches — Canadian English and American English — again each having regional and social dialects.[12]

English speakers in downtown Toronto, Kansas City, Glasgow, Singapore, Manchester, Memphis, Aukland, Jamaica or Capetown may find themselves in some funny and not-so-funny situations. A friend of mine, and a native Torontonian travelling through New

Delhi, India, asked several passersby for directions to the train station and no one knew what he was talking about. Finally, like a lightning bolt, it hit him: the British English word for train was "rail." Once he asked for the railway station, he got accurate directions, and even caught his train on time. The issue: Indian English is a branch of British English and Canadian English a branch of North American English, and ne'er the twain shall meet. At least not this time.

For English speakers living even in the same country — Canada, the U.S., Scotland, Trinidad or Australia — all communication is cross-cultural, based on where we grow up in a country (urban or rural), our ethnic backgrounds, our religion, our gender, our education. All of these things create our perception of the world and the kind(s) of English we speak. I remember a funny incident many years ago in cottage country in Northern Ontario. It was a Saturday night and I was "chowing down" on chicken wings and fries with my then husband outside a local pub. One of the regulars half turned to me and, in an amiable northern drawl said, "How's she goin'?" I took a quick look over my shoulder, saw no "she" in sight, so I somewhat hesitatingly said, "Fine thanks, you?", and our conversation continued. My Japanese ex-husband, however, in total confusion over the "she" pronoun, spent the next three minutes searching for the absent she. The issue: this gent greeted me in his colloquial, rural, non-standard dialect which used "she" for the standard "it" in "How's it going?"

Language and Culture

The language a person speaks transmits the attitudes and beliefs of that person's specific cultural group. So much so, that language and culture are intertwined and inseparable. During my year's stay in Japan, I found that when I asked Japanese students to answer a question, and the students wanted to make sure they were the ones I was addressing, they strategically placed a finger on their noses, nodded their heads, and looked to me for confirmation. A Canadian or American student would have asked, "Do you mean me?" or something to that effect. Japanese avoid using "I" or "me" because they operate with a "we" collective and at the same time, pay deference to the speaker. With this knowledge, I was able to enhance my communications capability and eventually share mindsets with my students.

LINGUISTIC COMPETENCE AND PERFORMANCE[13]

Synergistic human nature being what it is, allows us many language options. In spite of our linguistic competence (what we inherently know about language, sounds, words and rules for combining the chunks), our linguistic performance doesn't always reflect this knowledge. For example, even though we know the language, we may choose not to join the conversation or to purposefully leave out all our descriptive words when speaking with someone whom we know "likes things short." (We will discuss this short delivery style with the Lion in Chapter 5.)

In other words, knowing is not the same as doing. Here the gap between knowing and doing is a conscious one. Sometimes, the gap between knowing and doing is also unconscious. We all make mistakes when speaking — slips of the tongue and false starts. The term "spoonerism" was named after Reverend Spooner (1844-1930), a professor at New College, Oxford. He frequently entertained his students with gems like you "hissed my mystery lecture" for "you missed my history lecture" or "a well-boiled icicle" for "a well-oiled bicycle." My best spoonerism was starting an important presentation where I nervously asked everyone to please "shit down" instead of "sit down." These are performance errors and we have the knowledge to recognize them for what they are. They also can be fun and sometimes a tad embarrassing.

THE STYLE GAP

To speak to people in the way they most prefer, we first need a solid awareness of language to enable us to recognize what different people prefer. Based on these language preferences, listeners may very well listen differently. As well, differences in speaking styles (Chapters 5 and 6) can create either solidarity or an abundance of confusion, hurt feelings and miscommunication.

In science, for every action in a process there is a reaction or outcome. In word interactions, too, for every dialogue there is a reaction or outcome that we have complete control of: our response. Learning to work effectively with our speaking style differences and learning to close the "style gaps" is critical to communication.

As we saw in Chapters 1 and 2, what we expect of ourselves and what others expect of us can be at odds. Add the complexities of our speaking style gaps and communication becomes challenging. Thought and language work hand in hand, so we need to use our differing expectations together with our linguistic competence (what we know about language) to manage our overall performance style (what we do with what we know).

THE FEATURES AND TOOLS OF LANGUAGE

Debates on the origin of language and its function(s) in society are almost as old as language itself. Linguist Otto Jespersen (1860 to 1943) theorized that language came from song and that we used language to express community, sharing and love. If true, then as humans we would naturally want to create greater harmony in all our interactions. So, to help us close any dialogue gaps, we need to appropriately use the three features of language and the three tools of talk.

In the upcoming chapters on the Six Speaking Styles and the Six Challenging Personalities, we will see how different speaking styles and personalities reflect these features of spoken language and contribute to the many layers of meaning in any message. And it's these different expectations, perceptions and usage of these features and tools that contribute to either creating understanding between people or multiple miscommunications. It is easier to react rather than to respond to someone's use of language without really understanding what you are doing or why you are reacting that way. You just do it.

THE THREE FEATURES OF LANGUAGE[14]

Let's begin with a look at the three features of spoken language: (1) intonation and pitch; (2) pacing and pausing; and (3) volume. Then we'll turn our attention to the three tools of talk: solidarity of language, solidarity of likemindedness and solidarity of expression.

---

1. Intonation and Pitch

When you speak, your vocal pitch rises and falls. There are gender differences in pitch (women have higher-pitched voices) as well as personal varieties. Intonation reflects our pitch and the other language features of pacing, pausing and volume (see below).

Through the features of intonation and pitch, we can place emphasis on words, phrases and sentences. These features clarify both the content message (the facts) and the relationship message (the feelings) and are used to signal a shift in speaker at the end of a sentence.

Intonation, Pitch and Perception

People will often shift their pitch to make their message clear; for example, they will drop their voice on "Oh" to show disappointment or use a high-pitched "Really?" to show surprise. Have you ever called someone at the "wrong" time and the person shifted his pitch to let you know? This happened to me when a colleague put extra emphasis on the "what" in "What can I do for you?", which implied that it wasn't a good time for him to talk.

If you expect big shifts in others' intonation (for example, to show the highs — excitement, passion, enthusiasm — and the lows — hurt, stress, anger) and don't get them, you will be disappointed. Some people become very quiet when they're angry. Others have exploding intonation. Some people have a constant intonation pattern that rarely varies, good news or bad. These monotone speakers can be difficult to understand sometimes because you're not sure what they are thinking and feeling.

In Latin America, there's a great variety in pitch and intensity for all expressive reactions. If you show little vocal range, you would be viewed as unemotional, even repressed. The bottom line is that intonation and pitch, regardless of what language, convey meaning.

I remember working with a Japanese teacher when I lived in Tokyo. When she spoke English to me, she had well-modulated pitch. However, when she spoke Japanese with her male counterparts, her pitch rose several octaves and her voice sounded almost child-like. She also constantly used rising intonation at the end of her sentences, whether they were interrogatives or not. To an English speaker, this ongoing intonation pattern showed a level of uncertainty and a need for validation of her ideas and thoughts. It also greatly affected the intelligent content of her message; in lieu of giving information, she now sounded like she was seeking approval. When we talked about this, she was aware of the shift in her intonation pattern and was bothered by it. Nevertheless, when she spoke Japanese, she immediately reverted to her old pattern or The Dance Trap — one that is (at least was in 1984) expected and accepted for Japanese women.

2. Pacing and Pausing

When you speak, your pace varies from ultra slow to ultra fast, based on the individual. We change the pace in our conversations to give variety, to signal interest, to show appreciation, to demonstrate active listening (we might slow our pace to show caring and speed up our pace to show enthusiasm), and to establish rapport with our partner in dialogue. "Match, Pace, Lead" (MPL) is a useful technique we will discuss to establish rapport through pacing.

We pause intermittently during our sentences for emphasis and to give the listener an opportunity to interject. We also pause at the end of a sentence for different lengths of time. Everyone has a different "pause gap." Some of us, like me, are "short-gappers." Others practice a medium-length gap and some have a long gap. Pause gaps at the end of a sentence signal the listener to speak.

Pacing, Pausing and Perception

"A pause in the wrong place, an intonation misunderstood, and a whole conversation went awry."

- E.M. Forester, *A Passage to India*

People have different perceptions and expectations related to pausing intervals and pacing in a conversation. Often, these expectations are unconscious. Some people like a short gap between the time one speaker ends a thought, and the other starts. For others, longer gaps are habitual, which is generally associated with politeness. If a speaker is having difficulty finding the right opportunity to interject in a conversation because of a perception of politeness he or she has, the ramifications are endless. Opinions galore are formed and questions arise, such as, Does he or she lack knowledge? Is he shy? Does she need assertiveness training? Was he not paying attention? Does she have nothing to input? Is he a slow thinker?

Conversely, if the speaker is perceived to be moving in too quickly to get his turn at talking, is he labelled as pushy, rude, selfish, inconsiderate, insensitive, impolite, insecure or aggressive? Any and all labels are possible but not necessarily helpful. Or what may be happening is that the person has a short gap pause. Your pausing and pacing patterns, then, can create an image for the other person that may or may not have some basis in fact.

To help people better understand how they pause and pace, and what others expect in this area, I often use what I call "the Interruption Ball" in my workshops. To speak you have to be holding the ball, and to get the ball you have to ask for it — either verbally or non-verbally. What I have found is that for people who have a longer gap (they like a longer pause), asking for the ball is a welcome relief. The few seconds that elapse between speakers makes them feel comfortable. Short-gap pausers are frustrated by the ball because they have to wait to speak. This is good practice for everyone to understand how language chemistry works and how comfort is formed. And as a short-gapper myself, it has certainly helped me. I've been told on more than one occasion that I "cut people off quickly," especially on the telephone. One technique that helps me to lengthen my gap at the end of a sentence is to do a three-second count before I begin another sentence. This also gives the other person ample time to interject and I avoid sounding abrupt which can easily be misinterpreted as rude.

As well, if you want to speak you can signal this through a head movement, by leaning forward, by sitting straight up. You might use a hand gesture (raise, and wave) increase or decrease your volume, or simply ask to have the floor. This shift in your style will immediately stop any style clashes you and your partner may be having. If both people speak quickly and use a short-gap pause system — "duelling banjos" as I call them — they can easily cut each other off and burn each other out. So, shifting can be a very valuable tool. When I'm in a duelling banjo situation, I generally slow the pace down and go with longer pauses (three-second count), allowing both of us an opportunity to create a new rhythm in the conversation.

Match, Pace, Lead (MPL)

A colleague of mine once had lunch with a friend and his client. Upon introductions, the client immediately labelled my colleague as "a competitor" and told her so. She had no idea what he was talking about, but it was clear to her through his speaking style and body language that he felt threatened. In response, she assumed a laid back approach, graciously shared the floor amongst all, slowed her naturally quick-paced speech to match his slower pace, and left pause time at the end of sentences. By doing a style match, she was able to help him overcome his feelings of insecurity and create the positive, unthreatening atmosphere necessary for effective communication. "Match, Pace, Lead" (MPL) is a helpful technique to create harmony between speakers who have different pacing and pausing patterns.

Deborah Tannen (1986) described a technique that worked for one of her students. Student A was constantly cut off in conversation by Student B. To manage the conversation, Student A decided to immediately cut off Student B in return. When Student B raised her voice, so did Student A, and so Student A was able to control the conversation throughout.[15]

A level playing field was created between speakers through this theatre technique called "topping." As you can appreciate, you would vary the technique based on the people and the situation. It would not work with some kinds of people, and I also think it could be quite tiring if carried on for too long.

We think much more rapidly than we speak and people who think quickly may, or may not, speak quickly; some people naturally speak more quickly, others more slowly. Slower speakers can find a quick pace intimidating, so fast pacers need to be aware of any clues in the listener that tell them to slow down. My strategy, when I lived in Japan and travelled in South-East Asia, was to slow down my pace and to leave longer pauses between sentences to make my partners in dialogue comfortable. Except in Hong Kong, of course, where I had to speed everything up two notches just to keep up!

3. Volume

When you speak, you naturally vary your level of loudness. We use this feature of language for emphasis, to signal a shift in speaker (you can either increase or decrease your volume), and to convey a variety of feelings.

Volume and Perception

Some people speak louder when they make an important point. Others either increase or decrease volume to signal the other person to speak. And others use volume to indicate heightened emotions of excitement or anger. Equally, if a point is not so crucial, someone might turn down the volume. And often for sensitive issues, loudness can again decrease almost to a whisper. In some cultures, we decrease volume to show respect for people we may consider status bearers (parents, elderly, professors, doctors).

If someone is louder than we expect, we might perceive them as angry or pushy. They might even scare us a little. If they are softer than you expect, we might think them reserved, unassertive or lacking in confidence. Some angry people keep the volume down and show their anger in their sarcastic or biting tone. Others who are angry don't talk at all, and they use silence to indicate just how angry they really are. Whatever system the person has in place (and it is just that a system), it's logical and works for him and it may be quite different from your own. In Japan, I always decreased my volume as I found Japanese in general to respond better to soft-spoken speakers. I increased my volume in South America to show interest.

THE THREE TOOLS OF TALK

Both consciously and unconsciously, people use a number of linguistic tools to establish relationships and build solidarity. These tools are unique to each person's perception of how people share and care. And remember, as we discussed in Chapter 1, both sharing and caring are inherently ambiguous, so this allows for multiple interpretations and misinterpretations.

The three tools of talk we will look at are:

1. Solidarity through Language
   a. jargon
   b. personal anecdotes
   c. indirect communication
     - politeness
     - subtlety.

2. Solidarity through Likemindedness
   a. common ground
   b. good news
   c. bad news
   d. gossiping
   e. complaining
   f. apologizing.

3. Solidarity through Expression
Created through intonation and pitch, pacing and pausing and volume which creates a range in expression from subdued to intense.

1. Solidarity through Language

Using Jargon
In everyday conversation, we share and communicate through the words we choose. For example, two human resource professionals or two engineers will enjoy the common language or jargon of their respective fields and immediately have a bond. In a lovely *Bizarro* comic by Dan Piraro, two off-duty mechanics illustrate these common language bonds:

> Mechanic 1 (leafing through a magazine): "... This new Corvette article at first glance seems pedantic and heavy-handed, but the subsequent introduction of an altruistic

approach to the suspension and steering mechanism enables it to surpass and transcend the usual sports car rhetoric."

Mechanic 2 (on a nearby bench): "... Thank Heavens."

I'm not sure "exactly" how off-duty mechanics sound but you get the idea. I also had an interesting experience where a term in a technical department was assumed to have the identical meaning for all, but did not. Quality improvement technicians from each of the department's four sections had a different definition for the word "bulk," based on their role in the quality improvement process. For example, "bulk" to the group at the start of the process meant raw material. "Bulk" to the group at the end of the process meant the weight of the finished product. So, when they talked to each other about "bulk," although they meant different things (and this often caused confusion), each group worked on the premise that "bulk" had a common meaning for all. In the workshop, the teams were able to share their "bulk" definitions and in doing so gain a greater understanding of their co-workers' role in the quality process.

In addition to the language bonds created through the features of language (intonation and pitch, pacing and pausing and volume) and through jargon as in the previous examples, we use other parts of language to form bonds; for example, stylized humour in the forms of metaphors, puns and witticisms, and frequent alliteration to create language bonds. Colloquialisms, clipped wording and not-so-perfect grammar, for example, can create camaraderie. If we want to establish a common language for a conservative relationship with a client or business associate, we might slow down our pacing, keep our grammar formal, not clip our words, and slowly ask questions rather than toss them out (a sign of camaraderie). Think about your relationships with people at work and with your friends. You've probably formed language bonds whether you're aware of it or not.

If you sense that a person is reticent in dialogue, do a spot check (as discussed at the end of Chapter 3) to see where the problem may lie. They might think you're being too direct or too intimate too soon, and might feel more comfortable if your style imitated theirs a little more.

Using Personal Anecdotes
Another linguistic tool people use to bond is the use of multiple personal anecdotes or self-revealers. (This is a favourite of the

Chimpanzee we will meet in Chapter 6.) They beseige you with one personal anecdote after another with the expectation and hope that you will chip in and start talking about yourself, just as they do. Have you ever gone out on a first date and the other person floods you with story after story about himself or herself? Believe it or not, this may be an attempt to get to know you, although it appears to be at cross purposes.

I once had a business associate ask me why I didn't talk about myself as he did. In his mindset, people who talked about themselves all the time were "successful." I shared neither his mindset nor his anecdotal style. Your options are to match the person's style or model your own style for the person, in the hopes he or she catches on (if you can get a word in, that is). Anecdotal types can totally turn some people off because they are thought to be self-absorbed and arrogant, talk too much, are too direct, insensitive or just plain rude. As well, this "overflow of information" is often perceived as inappropriate in the early stages of getting to know someone.

Through language, our goal is to find that common rhythm that both parties feel comfortable with. Have you ever danced with someone and had to adjust your rhythm more than once to keep afloat, to keep the beat or to avoid stepping on toes? Well, dialogue mechanics require the same kind of give and take, push and pull. Dialogue represents a constant balancing and rebalancing to meet both parties' needs for community and autonomy. In plain English: it's important to know when to shut up.

Indirect Communication

Indirect communication is used as a marker of politeness and subtlety. A way to firmly and indirectly make your point. Let's look at the following examples.

EXAMPLE

"One great use of words is to hide our thoughts."

- Voltaire

Friends Mark and Rachel are reading through Mark's poetry and short story collections on disc. Mark is delighted to share his work with a friend and fellow author, and asks Rachel if she'd like his work on a couple of discs. Rachel readily agrees. Mark then tells Rachel that he uses "very high-quality discs." At first, Rachel doesn't get it; then as Mark appears more uncomfortable when he talks about making the discs, Rachel realizes that

Mark wants her to provide the discs and she agrees to drop a couple off.

However, a couple of weeks later when Rachel speaks to Mark on the telephone, Mark says that he's not finished making the discs. Rachel is surprised, says there must be some kind of miscommunication because she agreed to drop off the discs. Mark then readily takes her up on her reoffer and says, "Okay, let's leave it at that." Rachel drops off the discs and Mark prepares them for her.

ANALYSIS

(a) Mark did not hear/listen to/understand Rachel's direct communication to provide the discs (perhaps Mark was feeling "put upon" and put his Self-Protector listening mask on)

(b) Mark forgot that Rachel had agreed to provide the discs (unlikely, however, as he started the conversation by telling Rachel he hadn't finished yet with the hope she would reoffer)

(c) Mark changed his mind for whatever reason(s) and decided to provide the discs (unlikely as he was clear in his message from the start)

(d) Mark had always intended for Rachel to provide the discs and was relieved (because he didn't know how to discuss the problem) and immediately agreed when Rachel "reoffered" to provide the discs.

WRAP-UP

I believe what happened here was a combination of (a) and (d). Rachel had agreed to provide the discs, but Mark was not 100 percent sure of this. So again Mark used indirect communication to bring up the topic, hoping Rachel would reoffer, and she did. Following are Rachel's comments about the incident: "It took me a few minutes to understand that Mark wanted me to drop off the discs. With close friends, we automatically do this for one another and would never ask to be 'paid back' for the cost of a couple of discs. If the discs Mark uses are expensive and of a higher quality than needed, he could have easily picked up less expensive discs to use. I never would have known the difference. *But Mark is cheap, and just couldn't be bothered.*"

Indirect communication, contrary to popular belief, is not dishonest — rather it is another linguistic tool to communicate your ideas and your relationship by saying what you mean but "not in so many words." Other examples of indirect communication include:

- not saying "no" but meaning no
- not saying "yes" but meaning yes
- hinting at something without actually talking about it
- picking up on hints or cues that someone is dropping
- choosing to think something, transmit the message but not state it directly
- surmising what someone else means when they choose not to state the message, for example when a teenager asks if she can borrow the car to go to a movie with a friend and her mother gives no answer. From the silence the daughter surmises that she can go, and that her mother will also throw in gas money!

Here's another example from my personal experience. During the course of writing this book, a "friend" asked me if I would be acknowledging certain "people" (meaning his wife) in my book. I took an uncustomary longer gap in my pause and answered, "Absolutely, every one who contributed." My response was both indirect and ambiguous.

Understanding Beyond the Words

"There was speech in their dumbness, language in their very gesture."

- William Shakespeare, *The Winter's Tale*

Indirect communication also encompasses the whole realm of message-making components; namely, the words, verbal and non-verbal elements we looked at in Chapter 3 to form both the content message and the relationship message. In the following example, indirect communication helped Andy decide to let the conversation go.

EXAMPLE

Andy and Carter had an argument. Andy visited Carter to apologize. After Andy explained what had happened, Carter said in a quick-paced voice, hands tapping, "Anything more?" Andy responded, "No."

ANALYSIS

Although Carter chose the "right words" to encourage further dialogue, Andy got a different message — that he truly didn't want to talk about it any more. Carter's tone of voice, controlled facial expressions and hands suggested to Andy that he should move on to something else.

2. Solidarity through Likemindedness

Using Common Ground

I got my wonderful Abyssinian cat from a breeder who had 10 in tow. When the breeder walked through my kitchen, he took a long, hard glance at the cupboards above the refrigerator and said, "You might like to empty those." With total curiosity and naivety (I was to be a first-time cat owner), I asked, "Why might I want to do that?" He answered, "Well, my cats like to sleep up there, and yours might like it, too." I responded with a nod and a smile. (Secretly, I thought he was nuts.) But I understood the bond he was trying to create through this scenario of likemindedness, of having common ground and I appreciated his effort. (I also kept my cupboards firmly shut.) Likemindedness between people is established through the sharing of common ground: shared interests, ideas, hobbies, values, similarities and humour, good and bad news, gossiping, complaining and apologizing.

Using Good and Bad News

Some people bond through the sharing of either good or bad news, or both. Intimate friendships and relationships, of course, combine a healthy sharing of good and bad. In doing so, likemindedness and camaraderie are created. In sharing good news, it presupposes that people are happy for each others' successes and wins whatever they may be. In sharing bad news, we hope to share the problem or pain, perhaps identify with the other person and gain some support.

Whether in the sharing of good or bad news, when the listener doesn't meet your performance expectations, a gap arises. For example, I remember when I first started my business, telling a friend about a communication strength I was happy about — the ability to cold call just about anyone and not feel rejected when he or she wouldn't see me. And to just keep going. Her response was a very curt and despondent, "Not everyone can do that." Although her response was accurate, her tone and body language suggested that she took my comment personally. She thought of herself as well as others who aren't comfortable selling themselves. In feeling sorry for herself, she was unable to share in my success, and the bond I was trying to create didn't happen.

In a bad news scenario, for example, you might tell your friend how tight your finances are this quarter because of your newborn and your husband being laid off. Your friend responds that although she's never had a newborn, she knows what it's like to be strapped for cash and is supportive and kind, and solidarity is created.

Or you might share your bad news with someone who is inclined to criticize and give advice and call you a poor money manager. Because your expectation was a good-humoured "I know what you mean," a knowing glance or an empathetic nod, and this was not what you got, a gap arises and again an opportunity for solidarity is destroyed.

Here, the bad news sharer not only didn't have his original expectations met (Potential Crash Site #2) but might also feel put down and stupid for having shared the problem in the first place, especially with the "wrong" person. After hearing your "friend's" viewpoint, you may even have some doubts about your own money management skills (Potential Crash Site #6). As this was definitely intended as a personal slight, you may opt to ignore, punish or confront the behaviour. This incident would also be an opportunity to revise your expectations in future, to match what you now know this "friend" is and isn't capable of giving.

Using Gossip

In business and in life, people will often create solidarity through gossip. Information comes to life through the grapevine and allows for an informal venting of frustration, comparison making, blaming, sharing of jokes, curiosity seeking, and the sharing of observations. Gossipers are generally viewed as folks who don't have enough of their own business to mind, so they've poked their nose into other people's affairs. Nonetheless, they are experts at creating solidarity through likemindedness. Birds of a feather do flock together.

Using Complaining or "Kvetching"

In a *Hi & Lois* comic by Mort Walker and Dik Browne, we hear Lois complaining to her husband that she never gets to finish anything. Frustrated, she refers to her unfinished books, her needlepoint project, an unfinished letter that has been pending for four weeks, and her unbalanced chequebook. Finally, when Lois turns to her husband for solidarity, she finds Hi fast asleep, snoring away with a big smile on his face. Angrily, Lois says and "I never even get to finish complaining!"

When we complain or *kvetch* (the popular Yiddish word for complain), it presupposes a common view of the world, an opportunity to have your perceptions confirmed, and get some empathy, consolation or both. Decidedly an art form for some, it goes beyond the occasional complaint and is a morning, noon and night affair. To understand the ritual of complaining, we need to first distinguish between the four types of complainers:

(a) The Whiners: They look for solidarity through ritual complaining, are prone to self-pity and monologues but don't intend to burden or offend. They just want to be listened to (sounds like Lois).

(b) The Martyrs: They look for solidarity through ritual complaining and seek to gain approval and acceptance.

(c) Los Negativos: They *kvetch* for the sake of it, are unaware of their behaviour and create a negative spiral effect.

(d) The Takers: They *kvetch* for the sake of it, are aware of their behaviour and intend to satisfy their "I deserve" mentalities.

It's been my experience, that although there are a good number of complainers in the (c) and (d) categories (we will have a good look at complainers in Chapter 8 on challenging personalities), many complainers fall into the (a) and (b) categories and use the language ritual to simply connect. In this sense, complaining needs to be looked at as a ritual of human need — a way to create community.

Elevators I find cultivate the best ritual complainers. Often, they start with complaints about the elevator's mechanics: how slow the elevator is, how quickly the automatic doors shut or how long they always have to wait for the elevators in this building and would be better off taking the stairs. How rude people are pushing off and on. And on and on. Then, depending on weather conditions (and Canadians are notorious for this), they first establish solidarity by complaining about the outside weather conditions and then transfer this to the weather conditions on the elevator. Too hot. Too cold. Too dark. Too sticky. Speaking of weather, on the dog-sledding trip I mentioned in Chapter 2, we had a good deal of solidarity — in ice that is. We all had icicles hanging off our noses. And there was no solidarity in language as everyone's tongue was too frozen for talk!

Using Apologizing

Like complaining, apologizing allows us to create solidarity. When both parties follow "the rules of apology," the air is cleared and things can quickly be put back on track. Relationships can even become enhanced. However, when the rules are not followed, the original damage can be compounded as in the following example.

To end a disagreement, both parties must claim a stake in creating it. In the following example, Gregory matches Anton's apology with a dig and so goodwill is destroyed. Now, the issue of "fault" is again in question as Gregory lays blame and the original anger is incited all over again. Once again, solidarity is destroyed.

Anton (sincerely): Well, I apologize for misinterpreting your comment. Sometimes I am a little sensitive, and I do take things personally.

Gregory (sarcastic): Yes. I've noticed that on a couple of occasions.

Anton (angry): Thanks a lot.

Because people have different expectations of what "apologizing" looks like, the apology can take several forms:

➤ Clearing the air immediately by accepting someone's apology. This doesn't have to be in the form of verbal acceptance but could include a handshake, a hand on the shoulder, a nod of the head or a smile.

➤ Carrying on a conversation until the issue arises naturally in conversation or is brought up at an appropriate time and then is dealt with.

➤ Going "beyond words" in indirect communication — using intonation, pausing and body language to convey your apology without actually saying it.

➤ Dropping someone an apology note or a card, then following up as appropriate. Be prepared to take the initiative if you want to solve the problem.

3. Solidarity through Expression

Solidarity through expression combines your personal range of expression (intonation and pitch, pacing and pausing, and volume) with your partner's "range of expression."

When someone shares a wonderful piece of information with you, how do you express your enthusiasm? Your happiness for them?

Some people will eagerly respond with encouragement reflected in volume, intensity and pitch. But others may be put off by this enthusiasm. If your pace quickens and your voice gets louder, and you start to ask a bunch of questions, people might even wonder what all of the hullabaloo is about. And why you are getting so worked up.

As well, things could go completely the other way. If someone tells you a terrific piece of news and your reaction is subdued, they might think you are the Daydreamer, the Attention Faker B, the Selective or simply don't care. They might truly be offended at your lack of emotional display. Range in expression is unique to each person's way of being, is shaped by his language and culture, and the differences in style can lead to effective communication or miscommunication, as in the following example.

Example

Martin tells his "still new" friend Kevin about a dispute he had with a client who was not acting above-board. Kevin's response in words, tone and body language was *"That's disgusting."* Martin was startled by the intensity of Kevin's response, took it personally and began to doubt whether he'd handled himself all that well with the client. (This is a good example of Potential Crash site #4 plus a lack of awareness of Martin's Bull speaking style, which we will discuss in Chapter 6). Martin intended his response to show agreement and solidarity with Kevin for how Kevin handled the situation and "the disgust" they now jointly shared. However, the differences in range of expression between the two men created a miscommunication.

Summary

Walking the Human Tightrope

Our human needs to be part of the community and, at the same time, retain our autonomy have us walking a human tightrope in all our communication interchanges. We first move in to get close, then move away if we get uncomfortable. Good communicators always balance questions such as: How much do I ask? When do I ask it? What topics do I need to stay clear of? How close do I stand to this person? (20 to 24 inches is typical North American proximity). How loud do I speak? How soft? How intense? How calm? In an attempt not to appear intrusive or imposing, we pull back. In an attempt to be warm and friendly, we ask questions, move closer, show interest — but not *too* much interest. And we don't ask *too* many questions. And we don't get *too* close. Good communicators have to be the world's best tightrope walkers.

The Rope Was Too Taut

Ellen and Debbie met once six months earlier and have spoken on the phone a couple of times since. Now, working on a project together, they are having a quick lunch and an open conversation.

Debbie: You know I didn't really like you when I first met you. You were *so direct and sounded kind of hyper.* You asked so many questions.

Ellen: I thought you would appreciate the direct approach. As we had worked together some years ago, I was working on the premise that we actually knew each other a little. I am direct and enjoy being that way. I'm really not hyper just enthusiastic and sometimes I can get carried away. I ask questions when I like someone and I'm interested. I apologize if I offended you.

Debbie (thoughtfully): Oh. I understand *now*. No problem.

This example typifies where a good number of relationships stray from the start, and the expression he or she "came on too strong." And both Ellen and Debbie can learn from their mistakes; a more subdued Debbie was quick to negatively judge Ellen's expressive style without getting to know her first. Equally, Ellen made it difficult for Debbie to want to get to know her when she didn't adapt her style to better meet Debbie's comfort level. How we use the verbal features and tools of spoken language plus all the nonverbal dimensions of dialogue — gesture and body language, eye contact, physical distance, touch and smell and even clothing and jewellery — can make or break our relationships. This is how we bond or don't bond. And through a good understanding of these elements it can pave the way for enhanced communication.

Remember! Whenever you employ a linguistic tool in dialogue, and you don't get what you expect, revise your expectations and how you are using language rather than draw a negative conclusion about that person.

So Strategy 4 of the *How Not To Take It Personally Action Plan* is to know The Three Features of Language and The Three Tools of Talk.

Let's review the four steps to increase our knowledge and apply them.

1. Learn the language facts.
2. Look at both the content message and the relationship message you are sending to the listener.
3. Evaluate how you are interpreting and responding to the content message and the relationship message.
4. Experiment with the features and tools of language, and be prepared to switch gears to meet the needs of your audience.

CHAPTER 5

THE THREE PRINCIPAL SPEAKING STYLES

"Many of us expect others to look like us, talk like us, think like us and smell like us. When they don't, the tape in our head says 'They're doing it wrong.' We cling to these tapes as security blankets because moving out of our comfort zone causes us to feel scared and insecure."

- Terry Mosey, *Vice President, Sales & Service (Consumer), Bell Ontario, Bell Canada*

Strategy 5: ***Recognize and Interact Productively with the Lion, the Peacock and the Elephant***

What an intricate web we weave in the communication process! How we listen, interpret and respond to others is based on our perception, expectations, listening masks, and how we use the features and tools of language.

As a public relations consultant and English as a Second Language teacher, and later as a corporate communications coach, my interest over the years has always been in understanding what makes for "productive" communication. And in pinpointing where and why things had gone amiss, I often zeroed in on our own expectations, some very real language and culture differentials, how we listen, interpret and respond, and how we are perceived by others. As well, in my work, what became evident again and again is that there are three kinds of folks in the world: Navigators who see the big picture, Pilots who see the big and small pictures, and Passengers who see the small picture. This led me to look more closely at how people having these three different mindsets communicate. What I found is that there appear to be three principal speaking styles (the Lion, the Peacock, the Elephant) and three combination speaking styles, which we will look at in Chapter 6.

These speaking styles are a coming together of several disciplines and models related to (1) what people expect; (2) how they listen, interpret and respond; and (3) how they are perceived by others. Let me give you a little background to set the stage for the different speaking styles.

Psychiatrists Sigmund Freud (1856-1939) and Eric Berne (1910-1970), the originator of transactional analysis, worked on what they called Adult Ego States. In 1921, Swiss psychoanalyst Carl Jung, a Freudian disciple, produced *Psychological Types.* Jung's types included three personality preference scales and eight distinct personality types. In 1923, Katharine Briggs and her daughter, Isabel, pioneers of personality type, adapted Jung's model, expanded it and gave it practical application. In the current Myers-Briggs model, there are four personality preferences and 16 distinct personality types.

In the 1940s, the Myers-Briggs Type Indicator (MBTI), a test used to measure and evaluate psychological type was created and, over the years, personality types and personality profiles galore have mushroomed. Professionals in multi-disciplines and fields of work pay credence to the four basic functions Jung defined as thinking, feeling, sensation and intuition, and to the Myers-Briggs expanded model and its many adaptations. The Myers-Briggs personality model and various communication models allow you to become more self-aware. Other models based on social style help you learn about yourself based on others' perceptions of you.

An understanding of the principal speaking styles will translate into greater self-awareness and a better understanding of how others respond to your style. The styles also shed some light on how and why other people may not always readily accept your listening and speaking styles and how miscommunication can occur.

THE THREE PRINCIPAL SPEAKING STYLES

In understanding the speaking styles, it's important to realize that each style has characteristics that some will view as either positive or negative. We will discuss these characteristics in terms of strengths and growth opportunities for each style.* Similarly, none of the speaking styles is better or worse — they are just different.

* Note: The strengths and growth opportunities are based on my professional observations in my facilitation and coaching work.

And finally, remember that our speaking styles are forms of learned behaviour; therefore, people can choose to reframe, unlearn, relearn or change any aspect of their style provided (a) they are aware of a style's traits; (b) they want to make a change to the traits; and (c) they understand the change process they need to follow.

Let me give you a brief sketch of how each of the three principal styles functions.

1. The Lion
1. Mindset: Navigator — see the Big Picture
2. Focus: The Solution
3. Process: Tactical, solution-oriented communicators who thrive on leading and cutting to the heart of the issue to fix the problem
4. Delivery: Short

2. The Peacock
1. Mindset: Pilot — see the Big and Small Pictures
2. Focus: The Analysis
3. Process: Analytic, persuasive communicators who enjoy the synthesis of ideas and discussion for discussion's sake
4. Delivery: Long

3. The Elephant
1. Mindset: Passenger — see the Small Picture
2. Focus: The Feelings
3. Process: Intuitive, empathic communicators who nurture and want to be nurtured
4. Delivery: Medium-long

---

1. The Lion

Because of their Navigator's mindset, Lions see the big picture and create opportunities. They build. This group of communicator is often awesome and can be a challenge to deal with. What they all have in common is their ability to lead and to get the task done.

This task-oriented communicator cuts to the heart of any situation and calls it for what it is. And this isn't always easy for others to accept or like. In an attempt to be straightforward and to get the job finished, the Lion can be abrupt. Lions simply take charge of a situation — and make things happen. The Lion will share the stage, but only if you prove yourself a worthy partner. If not, the Lion can and will ride in and take over to get the task done.

Lions sound like this:

1. *When* will it be ready?
2. *How many* people are available?
3. I *need* to have final copy for the client for by 3 p.m. tomorrow.
4. *What's the budget?*
5. Are we going to be ready for the Regent Corp. meeting next Friday?
6. Are our targets set? *Have them on my desk tomorrow.*

A Communications Sketch: The Lion

1. How They Listen: Listening Masks

➤ Distractor B — a fidget widget gone bad who creates or gets caught up in the distractions

➤ The Self-Protector — erects a wall to shut the listener out

➤ The Selective — selects the information he wants to hear

2. How They Interpret and Respond

- Navigator: see the big picture
- are focused on the goal of the communication — "the solution" — and not the process
- tend to quickly absorb and respond to data
- handle direct feedback well
- can show impatience in clipped wording at sentence endings
- can sound abrupt as they generally are short-gap pausers and quick pacers
- state their opinions as if they were facts
- choose their words carefully to meet the audience, purpose, content and situation
- like to present the information in a concise, structured way and to receive it that way from others, too (solidarity through language)

- use shifts in intonation and vary their volume to create solidarity through range of expression
- cut directly to the heart of the issue and prefer direct to indirect communication
- are generally "straight shooters"

3. How They Are Perceived

- as having authority and credibility
- as taking charge of people, situations and the environment around them
- as people who make clear decisions, trust their gut and are assertive
- as strong and potentially intimidating
- as reliable and practical
- as good priority setters
- as aggressive, extreme and intolerant
- as intelligent and spontaneous

EXAMPLE

Roger (a Lion), the owner of a mid-sized manufacturing company, has teamed up with one of his partners to buy the third one, George, out. Negotiations were going so badly that Roger was almost certain they'd end up never speaking to one another, in addition to litigation.

Roger realized things needed to take a turn. He went home and talked through all the negotiations with his wife Anna. In three hours they reviewed all the facts and the feelings of the third partner that had come out in the negotiations. Anna's conclusion: Roger had not accepted George's issues and concerns as valid. He was solely focused on meeting his own needs; he'd discounted the needs of his partner.

The next day, Roger walked in and apologized to George, and he felt the weight of the world come off his shoulders. He asked George how he'd like to do things and at what pace he'd like to go. (Roger admits he's not a great negotiator and he can be quite a bully.) George then set the pace, was happy to meet the other two partners halfway and negotiations continued, leading to an amicable buyout.

ANALYSIS

Roger acted like an intolerant Lion in the negotiations (let's get the task done and now) while George was looking for some

understanding and acceptance of the things that were important to him. Small details, like the logos he'd designed for various clients, were an important discussion point for him in the
negotiations. Roger had ignored this detail as "little stuff"; he
didn't feel it was worth paying attention to, and in doing so had
ignored his partner's feelings. The relationship message Roger
was sending was "your feelings don't count." When the pain
got so great and a half a million dollars was on the line, Roger
made a concerted effort to become more tolerant and more
empathic, and to accept George's issues as valid. Once he did,
it led to a smooth buyout.

WRAP-UP

When I asked Roger what he'd do differently next time, he said,
"I'd start by being objective. Your sensing skills are very valuable, but not to the point where you've prejudged the other person. And that's what I did with my partner. We're different."

"Let's face it. We're all attracted to people who are like us.
At a cocktail party, to whom do you gravitate? The people who
are most like you. But in a relationship that is evolving, either
business or personal, you need to go far beyond questions like
'What's their station in life?' 'Where do they live?' 'Where did
they go to school?' 'Do our styles match?' And get to questions
that relate to mutual values and mutual business goals."

The Lion's Strengths

Charismatic
As enthusiastic communicators, Lions bring great energy to every-
thing they do, and this has vibrant spin-off effects for all involved.
It's easy to get caught up in Lion charisma.

Self-Committed
Lions understand that without self-commitment, nothing will get
done. Therefore, they look after themselves well and set up situations so as to fully look at all the options to make the best decision
for themselves and others involved.

Structured
Because Lions have the skill to envision the whole house from
blueprint to window dressings, they can always maintain a clear
focus and perspective of any situation — and get the task done.

Cuts to the Heart of the Issue
Lions can get to the heart of the issue. They can cut right to the
heart of a situation, take a clear tally of what's going on and make

a clear-cut decision about what action to take, and then take it. Although Lions will feel fear, they will always take action, work through the fear and come out on the other side.

The Lion's Growth Opportunities

Intolerant
Lions expect people to communicate with them using the same short, clear and direct delivery style they communicate in. When they don't "get back what they give out," they can become frustrated and appear intolerant, impatient, abrupt and rude.

Polaristic
Lions can see things as black or white, yes or no, good or bad, and have difficulty both seeing and accepting all the grey nuances in between. This makes them appear rigid, set in their ways and sometimes insensitive to "the little things" that frequently count a lot in decision-making and relationship building.

Undaunted
When Lions get ideas, they pursue them tenaciously, sometimes to the exclusion of other things. They can become obsessed with completing the task. High on persistence, they can be short on patience. Therefore, it's important when dealing with the Lion that you always be aware of the need for balance. It's easy to get caught up in the Lion's race and pace and get tired. This undaunted spirit can put some people off by making them feel rushed and unappreciated.

Intimidating
Lions are powerful in words and actions, and they can be seen as potentially intimidating by others who see themselves as less powerful.

Follow-up Questions

➤ List an example of a Lion you have successfully dealt with at work. How did you create your success?

➤ What strategies have worked for you when the Lion has become intimidating?

➤ In your experience, when does the Lion listen best?

➤ When giving a Lion information, what delivery styles work best for him?

➤ How do you handle an abrupt Lion?

➤ If the Lion isn't listening to you, what do you do?

2. The Peacock

These eloquently plumed communicators like to let you know what they know, how they think, why they think that way, and what they've accomplished. Constantly. Chronically. Intensely. They are masters at probing for data, synthesizing it and delivering it.

The Peacock, an analytic communicator, enjoys the words and the many lines of argument. Talking is part of a ritual of life that can take several forms: banter, analysis, lecture, persuasion, anecdotes, jokes, argument.

Peacocks sound like this:

1. Three years ago I returned to France *three times in one month*, actually over a three-and-a-half-week period, to meet the hectic demands of the business.

2. It looks like I'll be running *two companies* for the next few weeks, so scheduling might become a little tight and we might like to look at electronic meetings where possible.

3. In this *particular* instance, I believe the best possible choice is to ...

They love to discuss, to show off their verbal prowess and accomplishments, and want to be admired for it.

A Communications Sketch: The Peacock

1. How They Listen: Listening Masks

➤ The Selective

➤ The Mindreader — decides to mindread and not ask questions

2. How They Interpret and Respond

– Pilot: see the big and small pictures
– enjoy the logic and thought process
– gather and analyze details
– string ideas together
– lecture, debate and argue
– show conviction and state their opinions as facts
– talk a lot
– use a lot of words, and well
– enjoy descriptive language: puns, metaphors which they use to persuade and engage others

- prone to add extra and redundant information
- uses variety in intonation, pitch and volume
- are slower in their pacing and pausing than the Lion
- have a mastery of the words and create solidarity through language
- enjoy language subtleties and indirect communication, especially to create solidarity through common "intellectual" ground

3. How They Are Perceived

- as hard to persuade
- as wanting every detail
- as intelligent, controlling and credible
- as demanding (listen to and adopt my opinion!)
- as entertaining and charming when "they're on"
- as conflict avoiders
- as persistent: will come back to a point again and again to drive it home
- as having an affinity for and with words
- as people who trust the analysis but not necessarily their gut
- as intellectual power trippers

EXAMPLE

Gilbert, an entrepreneur in the communications industry, comments on how his team of Peacocks analyze a situation when they've lost a piece of business:

"If we're making a pitch and there's a competition between several companies, the client feedback often goes something like, 'We didn't think you were as creative as ...' or 'we didn't think you presented as well as...' or 'XYZ company spent much more time on ...'

"Our team always walks out angry. Hurt. Disappointed that we lost the business, and then they take jabs at the client. A typical comment might be: 'How ungrateful. Our presentation was first class, our introduction was superb, our technology impressive. What do they know? *We're the best — we don't need to compete with any other supplier.* I can't believe they didn't seriously consider our proposal. We gave them exactly what they asked for and then some. It's hard to believe the client didn't think our presentation was first class. We prepared immaculately for the presentation. And to tell us we weren't persuasive enough? How dare they?'"

ANALYSIS

Continues Gilbert, "The truth is that we didn't do our homework. We didn't really find out what the client needed and we didn't give it to them. *We didn't listen to the client.* We didn't listen to what they wanted and needed. We disappointed the client and lost the business — for good reason. We need to be angry with ourselves and no one else. We were too busy being impressed with ourselves and how good we were that we neglected to meet the clients' needs."

WRAP-UP

The Peacock is often so caught up in his own rhetoric that it is easy for him to put on the Selective and the Mindreader listening masks. In doing so, he can alienate his audience; no one likes to be lectured at or not really listened to. Everyone likes to put his opinion forward and to be listened to in a respectful way. To quote Hugo Powell, chief operating officer — Americas, Labatt Brewing Company Ltd., "The best way to listen to what people mean — not what they say — is to frame questions in ways that more astutely get people to say what they mean." Clearly, this team of Peacocks did not ask enough questions prior to putting together their presentation.

The Peacock's Strengths

Eloquent
As Peacocks enjoy "being heard," they have mastered a certain eloquence in style and tone. An air of credibility and respect surround them, and this, in combination with their linguistic virtues, can make them pleasing to listen to.

Persuasive
Well-versed in the art of persuasion, the Peacock has diplomatic skills, sociolinguistic versatility and a way with words. Peacocks are formidable opponents at the negotiation table as they have the skill to strategically lay out an argument to their best advantage. And Peacocks don't like to lose.

Strategic
Prone to in-depth analysis, the Peacock can strategically point out the facts and the feelings in any argument. Because they see things from their mindset only, they build a solid, determined case for

what they want. Things that appear inconsequential to a Lion (focused on the big picture) may easily appear very significant to the Peacock. The Peacock cleanses the surface and everything beyond that. A bit of quartz, that the Lion will automatically bypass, is a precious stone, a shining gem of potential argument power. And remember, the Peacock enjoys the challenge of winning against an opponent of equal skill and power.

Persistent
Peacocks go on and on until they get what they want. Their stamina is formidable and their persistence high. You have to eat a power breakfast before taking on the Peacock. And because they can be demanding and want your full attention, your listening masks may come in handy.

The Peacock's Growth Opportunities

One Mindset
Peacocks see things from only one mindset, so they can be difficult to work with. Others may view their inability to understand other mindsets as a lack of respect. Set in their ways, it is hard for them to switch gears and see it and do it another way.

Wordy
Peacocks can be bombastic and wordy, and this can sometimes turn some people off. It's often difficult to get your viewpoint across because the Peacock is a continuous record who doesn't like to be interrupted. This can be frustrating for the listener who wants to be an active participant too, but doesn't know how to cut in.

Arrogant
With a lot of information at his fingertips, the Peacock can be arrogant in style and tone, and will assume a power position rather than one of solidarity in any kind of debate or posturing. The listener can easily take this personally. No one likes to be talked down to.

Prone to Interruption-itis
Insistent on making their point, being understood and being admired for their eloquence in argument and style, Peacocks will sidestep, overtalk, interrupt, overcut — you name it — to keep their argument alive and thriving. The listener has to be assertive to get his point across and must let the Peacock know he's not being given equal air time and that the Peacock's behaviour could be considered rude.

Controlling
Maintaining control is of supreme importance to the Peacock. Without it, they feel frail and insecure. However, demanding con-

trol puts a real strain on any interaction and often the listener feels as if he has to sublimate his personality just to let the Peacock control the dialogue. This can have negative side effects in building relationships.

Follow-up Questions

➤ What's your first reaction in dealing with a Peacock?

➤ Do you cut them a lot of slack?

➤ Do you put on a listening mask to tune them out?

➤ When the Peacock is arrogant, what do you do?

➤ Peacocks will relentlessly hold their position in a debate. How can you encourage their flexibility?

➤ What is one effective strategy to deal with a controlling communicator?

Summary Dialogue: The Peacock and the Lion

Patrick (a Lion) is researching and writing his first quarterly financial report. Paul (a Peacock) is a business acquaintance and has offered to review the draft and give his input on the content and style. Experienced in this area, Paul thinks the report is timely, and he would like to contribute on a "no-charge" basis.

Paul, however, has a hectic schedule and has delayed Patrick's project by a week. Patrick is working on a firm deadline with his boss, so he leaves Paul a voice-mail message and asks if they can book a quick appointment to finish the draft. A day passes and Paul does not respond. Patrick calls Paul's office to ask if there is any way a message can be relayed to Paul. The office calls Paul at home, and Paul returns the call promptly. The conversation goes something like this.

EXAMPLE

Patrick: Hello.

Paul (annoyed, bothered and with a sigh): It's Paul.

Patrick: Oh hi, Paul. Thanks for calling me back. I tried to reach you yesterday and left a message.

Paul (annoyed and defensive): I got it *after* the end of the business day.

Patrick: Well, my boss has put me on a deadline, so I wanted to know if we could meet early next week for 10 minutes or so to finalize the draft.

Paul (air of control, like he's doing Patrick a favour): Well, I don't have my book with me, but why don't you call my office on Monday morning, and we'll fix a time for Tuesday.

Patrick: Great. Have a good week-end.

ANALYSIS

During the conversation, and after he got off the phone, Patrick felt uncomfortable and uneasy. He intended in no way to rush Paul or disturb him when he was away from the office. But he had a job to get done, and was both excited and nervous.

Let's review the facts.

1. Paul offered to help on the project at no charge.

2. Patrick waited an extra week to meet Paul's schedule.

3. Paul had not returned Patrick's original call; Patrick called again.

Let's review the feelings.

1. Paul showed annoyance and was defensive.

2. Patrick was persistent and focused on the task. Could Paul have perceived this as pushiness? Inconsideration? Being rushed? Lack of appreciation?

WRAP-UP

I believe this is what happened. When Patrick and Paul did get together to review the draft, the meeting went well "technically," but it was also clear that neither really wanted to work together again. They didn't really like each other's style. Has this ever happened to you? That you meant one thing and it was construed a completely other way? But no one brought up the issue and nothing was ever resolved?

---

3. The Elephant

Nurturing and being nurtured are the primary goals of the Elephant. As outstanding listeners and probers, people look to them for understanding, patience and acceptance. Loaded with many skills and talents, the gentle, soft-spoken Elephant works hard to bring out the best in people and to create harmony in any environment. Liking others and being liked are very important to them, and they make friends easily by being pleasant and showing interest in other people. They are very personal communicators, and their pace is slower and more caring. They are often underestimated by the other speaking styles, but watch out!

Elephants sound like this:

1. Well, *I'm really sorry* you feel that way. What can I do to help?
2. *I understand* what you mean. Let me see what our department can do for you.
3. *Together*, our team has the best chance at winning.
4. I know how you feel. It's been a challenge for all of us.

A Communications Sketch: The Elephant

1. How They Listen: Listening Masks

➤ They are superb listeners.
➤ They will only put on the Daydreamer and Faker A masks (unconsciously tuned out) when they are tired and can't listen anymore but don't want to hurt your feelings and tell you they are unable to concentrate.

2. How They Interpret and Respond

- Passengers: see the small picture
- are easily influenced and persuaded to see and take on another's mindset
  enjoy the communication process but are not solution oriented
- are not always honest with others and therefore can be hard to trust
- are open about themselves and their lives
- encourage others to tell them their problems
- qualify statements to avoid conflict
- use several techniques to gain insight and understanding, such as preparing, paraphrasing, restating (will be discussed in Chapter 7)
- avoid confrontation at all costs
- use indirect communication to avoid hurting people's feelings
- create language bonds through words that create solidarity: "share, us, sorry, together, deserve, we, our, team"
- have a slower pace and use longer pauses
- enjoy sincere one-on-one dialogue

- use personal anecdotes to build bonds
- are intuitive in picking up on others' body language

3. How They Are Perceived

- as people who give and look for support and encouragement
- as people who show constant solidarity, but not power, and can lack credibility
- as prone to blaming others as they are non-assertive and can be overly sensitive
- as flexible
- as pleasers who apologize for things and people not in their control
- as needing to be listened to
- as non-assertive and gentle in manner
- as pleasers who avoid telling the truth if it means hurting someone's feelings

EXAMPLE 1

Bob (an Elephant): Hi, Sara. How are you doing today?

Sara (tired and anxious): I'm okay, how about you?

Bob (notices Sara is much more low-key than usual): Are you sure you're okay? You're not your usual spunky self this morning.

Sara (smiling): Well, to tell you the truth, last night was a bit scary. Our neighbour's kid took a fall, and Luke and I spent half the night with them at the hospital.

Bob (concerned): I'm sorry to hear that. Is the kid going to be okay?

Sara: We hope so. Thanks for asking.

Bob (smiles): Take care. I'll check back with you later in the day.

ANALYSIS

Feelings-oriented Elephants will notice how someone is feeling and will find out if they can help. Bob demonstrates caring for Sara and her feelings and concern for the child who is sick. He probes gently and makes Sara feel comfortable and leaves her with a sense of goodwill through his compassion.

EXAMPLE 2

A mid-sized pharmaceutical company had gone through a series of major transitions over the last decade. The manager of the marketing department had reached a point where he was unable to continue to grow with the company, yet the president, who felt a great deal of loyalty toward this person, was unable to address the issue.

The president kept hoping that somehow "gold would be spun from straw," and if given enough time, things would improve. The president offered coaching, resources, time, everything — but nothing worked. He became frustrated and disappointed with the manager. Productivity continued to decline in the department until the marketing manager himself realized he needed to move on. When he did resign, the president's predominant feeling was one of relief.

ANALYSIS

The president is an Elephant who doesn't want to hurt the marketing manager's feelings by addressing his shortcomings.

But by avoiding the issue of looking at this person's current appropriateness for the job, he sets himself up for more disappointment and frustration. Once the marketing manager was replaced, the department flourished.

The Elephant's Strengths

Empathic
Naturally empathic, the Elephant is a truly active listener and can easily tune into others' mindsets and needs. Because Elephants are skilful at seeing others' problems, they can help others to counsel themselves through the rough spots. They're great hand holders.

Precise
High on detail, Elephants collect accurate data and are good at evaluating and organizing it. They ask insightful questions and get people to communicate honestly with one another.

Patient
Not quick to judge, Elephants will take their time to hear the other person out. They also take their time to think through the action/words to critically evaluate the best approach for each individual situation.

Harmonious
Elephants are primarily concerned with others' feelings, and they create a harmonious atmosphere where other people are comfort-

able and feel free to express themselves. They are experts at delivering bad news well and coaching people through their discomfort.

The Elephant's Growth Opportunities

Non-assertive
Lions, Peacocks and the others love to take advantage of the Elephant's gentle ways. Elephants will back down too easily in a conflict situation to maintain harmony — but never underestimate them. They're as big on retribution as they are on solidarity.

Non-authoritative
Elephants are sometimes seen as "touchy feely" or "wishy washy." Unlike Lions and Peacocks, Elephants are solidarity oriented and appear more laid back and less assertive. To ensure comfort, they are prone to say what they think the other person wants to hear, and some people find them lacking in credibility and hard to trust for this reason.

Prone to Avoidance-itis
To keep the peace, Elephants avoid conflict. They'll keep their true feelings and opinions to themselves, and can become frustrated. This symptom can surface in a number of ways and can stress a relationship. Because Elephants are more reactive than proactive, they don't always take advantage of all their opportunities and sometimes get run over by Lions and Peacocks.

Prone to Indecision-itis
Because creating a pleasant communication environment is critical to the Elephant, less emphasis is placed on making definitive action statements and setting concrete goals. Therefore, unwittingly, Elephants can hold themselves back from achieving both personal and professional goals in a timely manner and can create great disappointment for themselves.

Follow-up Questions

➤ List one situation where you got what you wanted from a Elephant.

➤ What is one good way to make an Elephant comfortable in a new environment?

➤ Indecision-itis prompted the president in the previous example "to hang in there." What could he do differently next time?

The Speaking Style Spot Check

1. What is your speaking style?
2. What is your partner's speaking style?
3. What aspects of your style are you comfortable with?
4. What aspects of your style might you like to work on?
5. What level of comfort has been established between you and your partner? (Notice your breathing, perspiration, degree of calm, degree of hesitation, degree of flexibility, degree of caution, ability to concentrate on what your partner is saying.) What level of comfort does your partner appear to have in each of these areas?
6. Is there something specific in the combination of your style and your partner's that is enhancing the level of rapport between you? (a) can you pinpoint it? (b) can you embellish it?
7. Is there something specific in the combination of your style and your partner's that is decreasing the level of rapport between you? (a) can you pinpoint it? (b) can you fix it?

Make any necessary adjustments in your style to ensure your partner's comfort. For example, if your style is direct (the Lion), do you need to be a little less direct to help an Elephant with whom you are newly acquainted to become more comfortable?

Remember! To get through to the Lion, the Peacock and the Elephant, meet their listening and speaking needs.

For the Lion: get to the bottom line and fast
For the Peacock: prepare a solid argument
For the Elephant: share your feelings

So Strategy 5 of the *How Not To Take It Personally Action Plan* is to know the three principal speaking styles: the Lion, the Peacock and the Elephant, and how to interact productively with them.

Let's review the four steps to increase our knowledge and apply them.

1. Decide whether or not you want to change anything in your style.
2. Review your experiences in dealing successfully with each style.

3. Focus on a particular strategy for each that has worked for you and practice it.
4. Run The Speaking Style Spot Check as needed when interacting with each of the styles.

THE THREE COMBINATION SPEAKING STYLES

"It's important to suspend your judgement and go in with an open mind when you first meet someone, especially if someone's style is different than yours. Once you get to know them, you might find out there are mutual values that you share."

- Greg Cochrane, *Chairman & CEO, Mariposa Communications Group*

Strategy 6:   *Recognize and Interact Productively with the Bull, the Chimpanzee and the Chameleon*

L et me give you a brief sketch of how each of the three combination styles function.

1. The Bull (combination style of the Lion and Peacock)

1. Mindset: Navigator/Pilot
2. Focus: The Solution and the Analysis
3. Process: Solution-oriented communicators who like to get the job done and who like to talk
4. Delivery: Medium

2. The Chimpanzee (combination style of the Peacock and Elephant)

1. Mindset: Pilot/Passenger
2. Focus: The Analysis and the Feelings
3. Process: Persuasive, intuitive communicators who like to talk and to make others feel comfortable

4. Delivery: Long

3. The Chameleon: Becomes whatever style fits with the audience, purpose, content and situation

1. Mindset: Navigator, Pilot and Passenger
2. Focus: The Solution, the Analysis and the Feelings
3. Process: Solution-oriented, analytic and intuitive communicators that choose an "appropriate" speaking style
4. Delivery: Short to Long

---

1. The Bull

The Bull is a combination style of the Lion and the Peacock. Articulate and intelligent, the Bull is prone to exaggeration, intensity and a flair for the dramatic. And bulls can get snorting mad when they don't get what they want. They will go to great lengths to prove their point and to win.

Bulls sound like this:

1. Building the business was a *grueling* eight-year experience, but I did it — and I always made time for my friends.
2. I'm certain that what you *meant to say is* ...
3. *Precise* communication is a necessary ingredient to the success of any exchange.
4. You *should* really make a career move now.

A Communications Sketch: The Bull

1. How They Listen: Listening Masks

➤ Attention Faker B — fakes attention
➤ The Self-Protector
➤ The Selective

2. How They Interpret and Respond

– Navigator and Pilot: see the big and small pictures
– are highly analytical with the bottom line in mind
– use big shifts in intonation and pitch which make them interesting to listen to
– use solidarity through expression — will show you the highs and the lows

- are assertive and cuts to the heart of the issue (and you)
- can be wordy and use language to bond
- are committed to telling others they are wrong if that is the case
- focus on winning
- enjoy being the devil's advocate in a debate
- like to lecture at you
- say what they think with a twist: they share their biases, shortcomings and what they like and don't like, in a human, personal way
- are prone to quick-paced speech, and will pause for dramatic effect and modulate volume
- use indirect communication that hits the mark
- create solidarity through the sharing of ideas and perceptions

3. How They Are Perceived

- as people who don't like to be wrong
- as not always able to accept responsibility for what went wrong in the interaction
- as intense communicators who can easily be misinterpreted
- as helpful to the point of being overbearing
- as smart and capable

EXAMPLE

Remember in Chapter 2 Nicole had mentioned that she was thinking of buying a house, and she suggested to Bernard that she view one in the project his team was designing. Well, Nicole put the project on hold for a number of personal and professional reasons.

But Bernard (a Bull) brought the moving issue up several times, telling Nicole that "she really should move." Nicole stated that it was not her priority at this time. Because Bernard felt he had Nicole's best interests at heart, he was relentless, and kept trying to make his point that "she really should move."

As a result, Nicole got angry because he was ignoring her feelings, and responded by telling Bernard she could give him a "long list of shoulds" if she wanted to. Bernard took this comment personally, became defensive and insisted Nicole "go ahead" with her list, adding that it didn't mean he would listen. He had put on his Self-Protector listening mask and wanted to let her know it was firmly in place.

ANALYSIS

Nicole had brought up the "should list" as a strategic tool to stop Bernard from advising her to consider moving, and it backfired. The truth was, Nicole had no list of shoulds for Bernard. When Nicole realized that her Bull tactic had failed (can there be two Bulls in one ring?), in true assertive Lion style she simply said "No," accompanied by a stop-sign hand gesture, and let the conversation die. Bernard accepted her definitive answer in true Lion fashion (remember the Bull is half lion and will respond to the Lion style) and they moved on to another topic.

Remember! "Shoulds" or unsolicited advice that a person offers to another can easily be taken personally. All of us like and need to be our own decision-makers. We will discuss this further in Chapter 7.

The Bull's Strengths

Oratorical
With the Lion's charismatic style and the Peacock's ability to visually present ideas, the Bull has the talent to be a professional speaker, facilitator, dramatist, courtroom lawyer, raconteur.

Competent
Confident and credible, the Bull is a polished presenter. The Bull's work is always immaculate in how it looks, feels and sounds.

Laserlike
Able to cut to the heart of the issue and to see a variety of mindsets, the Bull can present and project a smorgasbord of ideas in a clear, laserbeam-like way.

Structured
High in structural format and keen on presenting powerful word images, the Bull is also a formidable mediator and writer.

The Bull's Growth Opportunities

Intense
Prone to putting on airs and displaying their verbal talents, bulls can easily "shoot the bull" as part of their oratory. Tie this to their dramatic intensity and they can really turn you off — or on.

Prone to Interruption-itis
It's difficult to get a word in edgewise with the Bull. They can become obsessed with making their point. However, they feel it's just fine to interrupt you, and others can view this as a lack of respect.

Professorial
A keen lecturer, Bulls can be a real pain when trying to be helpful. In reality, Bulls very much want to help, but can appear pushy, all-knowing and arrogant in presenting themselves as supreme advice givers. Whether they are asked to give advice or not, they feel compelled to strategically point out what you should do and why you should do it. They want to be helpful and genuinely have your best interests at heart, but sometimes they can push too far.

Prone to Competition-itis
Bulls want and need to win, and they'll go out of their way to prove a point — that sometimes may not even be worth the effort.

Follow-up Questions

➤ List one example of a Bull you had to deal with, your communications strategy and the results.

➤ How did you feel dealing with this person?

➤ Was it easy to derail the Bull?

➤ Did you come to enjoy the Bull's intensity?

2. The Chimpanzee

The Chimpanzee is a combination style of the Peacock and the Elephant. A strategic, win-oriented, high-vocabulary communicator, this type of speaker can certainly keep the questions coming and the conversation going — ideally until he or she wins. Chimpanzees want to be seen as capable and eager and on top of things, and at the same time pay clear attention to the other person's feelings, which are very important to them.
Chimpanzees sound like this:

1. Well, I think that it would be *a great idea* if you joined us.

2. Actually, Bruce, I'd *love* your input.

3. I think if we *combined* our talents, we'd be able to produce a superior product.

4. I'd *really like to encourage* you to come out to our next product demo.

A Communications Sketch: The Chimpanzee

1. How They Listen: Listening Masks

➤ Attention Faker B
➤ Distractor B — decide to create or get caught up in distractions
➤ The Selective

2. How They Interpret and Respond

– Pilot and Passenger: see the big and small pictures
– enjoy small picture detail
– blend facts and feelings
– lead the other person to where they want to go
– provide a lot of data and can easily get off on a tangent
– enjoy the banter, like the Peacock, but like the Elephant, they are less honest in any attempt to avoid any hurt feelings
– ask probing questions
– use a lower volume and are wordy
– will come back to the argument more than once
– will back up an argument based on personal experience and the experience of others
– are quick pausers and pacers
– create solidarity through personal anecdotes and the sharing of common ground

3. How They Are Perceived

– as people who want to be liked
– as people who work to create a harmonious atmosphere, like the Elephant
– as know-it-alls
– as helpful and credible
– as persuasive and competitive
– as warm, friendly and easy to talk to
– as conflict avoiders who use indirect communication

EXAMPLE

Darlene (a Chimpanzee) and Alfred drop into Cafe King for a coffee. Darlene suggested the restaurant as it was convenient for both and Alfred willingly agreed. They both order coffee.

They have not seen one another in months and there is unresolved conflict.

Alfred (tasting his and in a tone of disgust): Cafe King *never* had good coffee.

Darlene (concerned): Why didn't you say something before?

Alfred (condescending and sarcastic): Because I guess it *wasn't important.*

Darlene (sincerely): If it wasn't important, why are you mentioning it now?

Alfred (belligerent): Well, I guess you're right.

Darlene (attempting a joke to lighten things up): It happens once in a while.

Alfred (sarcastic): I'm *glad* you said that.

ANALYSIS

Darlene was genuine in her concern over the "bad" coffee and in Alfred not being happy at Cafe King. She would have gladly changed restaurants. However, when Alfred responded sarcastically to her genuine concern, Darlene tried to avoid the conflict but Alfred just got more sarcastic. Even Darlene's disarming strategy (a joke) at the end had no positive impact on Alfred — or the interaction. Here, the relationship message blocked out the content message and all of Darlene's attempts at harmony were in vain.

WRAP-UP

Here, both Alfred and Darlene were disappointed with the interchange — Darlene because her original feelings of concern for Alfred and "good coffee" had been misinterpreted, and both because they'd resolved nothing. Alfred, too, was not happy with himself for becoming increasingly nastier.

The Chimpanzee's Strengths

Analytic
Quick probers and analyzers, Chimpanzees can get into another person's mindset quite easily. As a result, they are superior problem-solvers.

Clever
Having the Peacock's verbal dexterity and the Elephant's intuitiveness, the Chimpanzee is viewed as a credible and clever communicator.

Harmonious
As peacekeepers, Chimpanzees hold back on their honest opinions and feelings to keep the peace.

Humane
Keen to share things about themselves, strengths, foibles and mistakes, they have a very human appeal, and can be warm and friendly.

Persuasive
Because they understand the other person's mindset, they can be highly persuasive and can strategically set up solidarity of like-mindedness.

The Chimpanzee's Growth Opportunities

Me-Focused
Because they are focused on themselves, they can get carried away. Others may see them as self-absorbed and conceited.

Prone to Indecision-itis
They are capable of understanding a variety of mindsets and want to be fair to all sides, so it can be hard for them to make a decision. This can lead to wasted time, energy and self-hurt.

Prone to Interruption-itis
Dialogue is plentiful and it's hard to silence a Chimp. Equally, the Chimpanzee is quick to interrupt you when you're talking, which will make some very angry.

Self-Revealing
Sensitive and keen to reveal themselves to their audience, Chimpanzees can also leave themselves quite vulnerable and can be taken advantage of. They are the personal anecdote specialists we talked about in Chapter 4.

Follow-up Questions

1. Do you ever put on a listening mask when dealing with the Chimpanzee? If so, which one would be productive?
2. How do you deal with people who challenge you?
3. Are you competitive?
4. Do you effectively persuade people to see your point of view?

3. The Chameleon

The Chameleon switches easily between all the other five speaking styles or combines the Lion and the Elephant styles. As the name indicates, this is not the easiest style to spot. Chameleons portray different styles based on the people and the situation, sometimes leaving many people confused.

Chameleons sound like this (Lion and Elephant):

1. "I *understand* your situation, and I'm sorry about the complications. At the same time, we *promised* the client a Friday delivery date. How do you suggest we proceed?"
2. They can also sound like the Lion, Peacock, Elephant, Bull or Chimpanzee.

A Communications Sketch: The Chameleon

1. How They Listen: Listening Masks

They are superb listeners but won't always let you know what they do or don't find of value; they will "switch gears" to meet your needs.

2. How They Interpret and Respond

– Navigator, Pilot and Passenger: see the big and small pictures
– are direct, analytical and intuitive (skilled ones are all three)
– will combine the facts and the feelings to reach a conclusion
– will either put the task first or the person's feelings first (skilled ones do both) based on the situation
– can confront with kindness
– are terrific at getting information through probing questions
– can quickly adapt to meet the speaking styles of the other five communicators
– can be subtle and know when to hold back
– can cut to the heart and know when not to hold back
– will vary all the features and tools of language to fit the people and the context

3. How They Are Perceived

– as wanting to be liked but not at the expense of getting the job done
– as confident, credible communicators

– as people who draw on different strengths strategically and eclectically
– as a mystery when they switch gears
– as a paradox
– as political
– as people who will not always give their opinion
– as people who will not always take a stand
– as great poker players and will not let you know their true hand
– as confusing, not always on the up and up

EXAMPLE

Martin (a Bull) and Eleanor (a Chameleon) have a joint project and are enroute to the client site. Martin is driving and has one of his favourite tapes blasting. He is completely in his own world and is interacting only with the music. Eleanor doesn't appreciate his self-absorbed attitude but decides to wait until they arrive to say something to Martin as he looks troubled. Martin beats her to the punch.

Martin (preoccupied and frustrated as they exit the car): I have to apologize. I'm not here. I'm leaving for a business trip to Japan on Wednesday. There are complications. I'm *already* in Japan.

Eleanor (calm, firm with empathy): I understand and I'm sorry there are complications in Japan. *But today's Monday,* and we have a job to do here in Toronto.

Martin (smiles and nods in agreement, then begins to talk about the project).

ANALYSIS

A preoccupied Bull is not the most pleasant person to be around. Martin was so buried in his own thoughts, he could have very well been alone in the car. But Eleanor didn't take it personally. (If the Bull is disgruntled with you, you'll hear about it in no uncertain terms.) Eleanor is working on the premise that Martin is mentally working on accomplishing some task. Therefore, as a Chameleon, she has several options to employ to get the Bull to remove his Attention Faker B mask and 'fess up.

WRAP-UP

Using direct communication (e.g. Is there anything wrong? Is something on your mind?) is a Lion strategy. This brings the situation quickly to fruition. Adept Chameleons like Eleanor can be assertive (Lion) and empathic (Elephant) at the same time. This is good when dealing with Bulls because Bulls respond well to Lions.

Watching and waiting is an indirect strategy for Chimpanzees and Elephants. Because Eleanor is sensitive to Martin's feelings and she could see and feel that something was on his mind, she decided to give him some time and not immediately ask if there was a problem. This strategy is productive provided that "in waiting" Eleanor doesn't get hurt.

The Chameleon's Strengths

Authoritative
With knowledge of people and speaking styles at their fingertips, Chameleons are viewed as smart and powerful.

Eclectic
Bits of everything, the Chameleon like the Lion is a natural leader, at times like the Peacock, a thorough analyzer, and a nurturer like the Elephant. To be able to switch gears successfully, the Chameleon must be high on structure, high on analysis and high on empathy. Adept Chameleons are many things but they only choose to show you certain things at certain times.

The Chameleon's Growth Opportunities

Predictable
A paradox by design, other people find it scary to watch a Chameleon in different situations as they will switch gears as the situation requires. As well, people find it difficult to trust Chameleons, who they view as not having a constant or predictable speaking style.

Follow-up Questions

➤ How can you tune your awareness skills to spot a Chameleon?
➤ Do you easily trust Chameleons?
➤ What speaking style do Chameleons respond best to?

Remember! If you want to get through to the Bull, the Chimpanzee and the Chameleon, prepare to meet their listening and speaking needs.

For the Bull: state your point in clear argument form

For the Chimpanzee: pay deference

For the Chameleon: share facts, analysis and feelings

So Strategy 6 of the *How Not To Take It Personally Action Plan* is to know the three combination speaking styles — the Bull, the Chimpanzee and the Chameleon — and how to interact productively with them.

Let's review the four steps to increase our knowledge and apply them.

1. Decide whether or not you want to change anything in your style.
2. Focus on your strategy in dealing effectively with each style.
3. Ask yourself if you have any bad habits in dealing with any of these styles, and prepare to work at improving them.
4. Run the Speaking Style Spot Check (see Chapter 5).

The Success of the Interaction Is Up to You

Now that you've gotten to know the Six Speaking Styles and the Six Listening Masks, you should be feeling even more confident that you are in control of your communication options.

Have you ever piled the guilt high and blamed yourself for all the miscommunications that you've had with people? Or on the other hand, have you always put all the responsibility on the other person's shoulders and taken very little yourself? Well, from here on in, don't do either. You are 100 percent responsible for your listening and speaking styles. And you can focus the success of any interaction by getting a clear picture of your partner's listening mask(s) and speaking style. Once done, you are in a position to make good strategic decisions to get what you want, and set up a win-win for all.

In the next four chapters, we are going to make sure that you continue to hone your communication strengths and feel good about them on an ongoing basis. And in the event your dialogues have been riddled with hurt, irritation and disappointment, this won't be happening much anymore. You'll be responding — not reacting — and turning some potentially unpleasant or hurtful conversations into mutual successes. And where this is not possible, you will learn when to walk away and to not get hurt.

Summary of Part II: Create a Guide to Your Listening and Speaking Styles

1. The Six Listening Masks

➤ The DayDreamer

➤ The Attention Faker A or B

➤ The Distractor A or B

➤ The Self-Protector

➤ The Selective

➤ The Mindreader

2. Language Features

➤ intonation and pitch

➤ pacing and pausing

➤ volume

3. Language Tools

➤ jargon

➤ personal anecdotes

➤ indirection communication

➤ common ground

➤ good news

➤ bad news

➤ gossiping

➤ complaining

➤ apologizing

➤ range of expression

4. The Six Speaking Styles

➤ The Lion

➤ The Peacock

➤ The Elephant

➤ The Bull

➤ The Chimpanzee

➤ The Chameleon

Note which listening masks and speaking styles you use most often and which language features and tools are characteristic of your personal style. You might also like to do the same for any important people you interact with in business and in your private life. Keep this in mind as we move into implementation of your Communications Success Action Plan in Part III.

IMPLEMENT YOUR COMMUNICATIONS SUCCESS ACTION PLAN

CHAPTER 7

REAL COMMUNICATION TAKES WORK

"Unless you try to do something beyond what you already mastered, you will never grow."

- Ralph Waldo Emerson

Strategy 7: **Tune into Your 10 Communication Skills and Build on Them**

Now that we've had an opportunity to explore the Six Speaking Styles, we can focus on building our communication strengths to deal with any and every communication challenge, and to make each interaction a productive one.

You have identified your own speaking style, the listening mask(s) you are prone to put on, and how you use the features and tools of the English language, and now your mission is to build on your communication skills. And since skills are related to self-awareness, the awareness of others, mindsets and perceptions and expectations, we need to look back to the beginning of the book. We will be building skills in 10 specific areas:

1. Managing Expectations
2. Developing Effective Listening Habits
3. Getting and Giving Feedback
4. Dealing with Fear
5. Being Honest
6. Working with Anger
7. Creating Positive Confrontation
8. Making Decisions
9. Gaining Closure
10. Letting Go

Communication Skill Set 1: Managing Expectations

How to Design Realistic Expectations

As we saw in Chapters 1 and 2, when people's expectations aren't met, it can lead to various degrees of hurt and disappointment. This notion of hurt and disappointment related to expectations is compounded by differences in listening and speaking styles. To avoid this, how can you let someone know what you expect in an interaction?

The key to getting someone to pay attention to your needs means that you are prepared to give him or her the same consideration that you would appreciate. You also have to be prepared to adapt your expectations as appropriate to the situation.

I remember once going to a party on the evening after my car (the only one in the underground parking) had been vandalized. I was reluctant to park again in the underground lot, so I asked a relative of mine (who was also at the party) if he'd follow me home. His response was, "You're asking too much." Under the circumstances (I was scared) and because he lived only five blocks away from me, I thought my request was reasonable. He didn't. So I revised my expectations, got home safely alone and checked in with the party hosts to let them know I was okay. Was I disappointed? Yes. But I now knew how little this relative cared about my feelings and my safety, and what I could realistically expect of him in the future.

Create a Performance Contract

"Those people with the greatest expectations are the most vulnerable when their expectations are not met. I believe there are two main reasons this happens. As managers, we don't explain to staff what we expect of them. Then, when things don't go well, staff think they have some sort of personal deficiency and they are hurt and disappointed. We need to give people straw horses — a foundation, an outline, an example — to let them know how we want them to look at the project or assignment. As well, as managers we need to focus on the process rather than the person when things go wrong and we are giving feedback."

- John Howarth, *VP Sales — The Americas,*
Bombardier, Regional Aircraft

If we go back to the 13 Potential Crash Sites in Chapter 2, we will see that if we can come to agreement on expectations, then people can avoid becoming Crash Site Dummies. One way to do this is to establish a performance contract.

A performance contract between employer and employee helps to:

a) establish expectations on both sides
b) confirm whether both sets of expectations can't or aren't being met, and re-evaluate the opportunity for working together
c) design goals that each side will be able to meet
d) set regular times to re-evaluate the contract to ensure that the goals and needs of both parties are being met
e) opt out, if expectations can't or aren't being met.

Making Expectation Statements

One good technique to help avoid gaps in expectations is to clearly state yours. Following are examples of clear expectation statements.

➤ I need you to be at work by 8:00 a.m. every day.
➤ I want to talk about the report for month end.
➤ I want to review our roles in the upcoming publicity project.
➤ I need to know how you feel about working with Ben for the next three months.
➤ I want your opinion on the proposal before it goes to print.
➤ I need you to take the night shift for three weeks to cover the holiday crunch.
➤ I expect you to be ready for the month-end meeting two days prior so we can prepare the data for the team.

The Responsibility Gap

When stating your expectations, remember that it's the other person's responsibility to tell you if he/she can't meet your expectations. This will eliminate any hurt or disappointment up front and allow you to productively revise your expectations as needed.

Some speaking styles such as the Lion, the Bull and the Chameleon will find it easier to make assertive expectation statements of this kind. However, if your speaking style is the Peacock, the Chimpanzee or the Elephant, you will need to work on developing a similar statement style or develop your own strategy for transmitting expectations. One linguistic tool that can work well when two people are on the same wavelength is indirect communication (see Chapter 4).

What Are Realistic Expectations?

" Not everything that can be counted counts, not everything that counts can be counted."

- Anon.

Cathy, an in-demand interior designer, had done several thousand dollars worth of work on Michael and Sylvia's home. Sylvia asked that Cathy work on a mini-project that Sylvia estimated at about $50. It included the pickup, painting and delivery of a picture frame in the same colours as her daughter's room. The quotation came back at $300. Sylvia was shocked, upset and disappointed. Why hadn't Cathy come through for her in light of all the work they'd done together and the many referrals Sylvia had given her?

1. Did Sylvia have realistic expectations? Did she take this personally?
2. What are Sylvia's options for getting the work done?
3. Was Cathy's decision anything other than a practical business decision?
4. How could Sylvia and Cathy have reached a compromise?

Sylvia had an unrealistic expectation that Cathy "owed" her a favour. Cathy, on the other hand, didn't know how to show appreciation to a valued customer. As this was a small and time-consuming job for a "busy" Cathy, she made the price so unpalatable that Sylvia went away — angry.

Had the two been willing to reduce their power and enhance their solidarity, they could have reached a compromise with Sylvia dropping off or delivering the frame to Cathy. Then Cathy could have done the work at a reasonable fee, in between projects, and Sylvia could have arranged to pick the frame up when it was ready.

EXAMPLE

I've been going to my dentist in Toronto since I was 19. That's a long time. When I lived in Japan, I'd been "encouraged," shall we say, by my new dentist to do "preventative restoration work." Fascinated by the process, and terribly naive, this resulted in a collection of inlays (high-quality silver restorations that are inserted over a filed-down tooth). Since my return, over the last 10 years my inlays have popped off a couple of times (the glue wears out).

Each time one of these little guys fell off it cost me $50. When I talked to my dentist about it, he felt the price was reasonable. I didn't. I took it personally; I'd been with him for a long time and he wouldn't give me a break on the price for a recurring problem. When I checked on prices, his were not out of sight, but I could definitely have gotten a better deal elsewhere. So I had to re-evaluate both the facts and my feelings by asking myself some important questions.

ANALYSIS

1. Do I trust him? His opinion? Judgement? Work?
2. Am I satisfied with the quality of his work?
3. In an emergency, is he available?
4. Is he open to discussion on important dental issues?
5. Does he have my best interests at heart?
6. Is he conveniently located?
7. Is it easy to book an appointment?
8. Are his prices comparable?
9. Is he friendly?
10. Do we both feel a sense of loyalty and commitment?

WRAP-UP

I determined by systematically working my way through the questions that money wasn't everything and that I had an unrealistic expectation that he would be able to lower the price for me. Then I did one more thing that clinched my decision; I called him to discuss my inlay situation by phone prior to booking my bi-annual appointment. He called me back promptly and we reviewed the situation. I was certain, then, that I was comfortable with his skill and judgement, and that I didn't want to change dentists. (But I still don't like his prices.)

Defining Expectations in a Personal Relationship

Harriet made a new business friend named Pauline several years ago. Following is Harriet's interpretation of the situation.

"I thought Pauline was smart and funny and I was delighted that this new person had come into my life. I began to share some personal things with her. Very quickly she put me on hold, told me she had all of the 'close friends' she needed, and that she was not looking for any new ones or for an intimate friendship of any kind. I was disappointed; I had been hoping to make a new friend, and I felt quite sad for her that she had no room in her life for any new friends."

Pauline was very clear on what she wanted out of the relationship, and this allowed Harriet to quickly revise her expectations and resume their relationship as business friends. Although a little sad, her disappointment was minimal.

Remember! The more you learn about the person and the situation, the greater the opportunity to further define and refine your expectations.

Communication Skill Set 2: Developing Effective Listening Habits

"The road to the heart is the ear."

- Voltaire

In Chapter 3, we squashed the listening myths, identified the 12 listening facts and learned about the six listening masks. In Chapters 3 through 6, we also looked at opportunities to take our listening masks off and to help others do the same to move a situation forward. Here, we will look at specific listening skills enabling us to create a productive interaction regardless of the person's speaking style or listening mask.

The Eight-Step Program for Becoming a Better Listener

Step 1: Listen to Yourself

To build self-awareness, make the time to really listen to yourself. To what you want, need and feel. Avoid coping strategies like crying, eating, smashing a squash ball, taking a walk, exercising, thinking about or analyzing an incident again and again — unless you are really listening to yourself and looking for answers. Coping strategies are short-term panaceas unless you are truly listening to yourself.

A guide to listening to yourself:

a) Ask yourself what you are feeling.

b) See if you can be specific.

c) Notice what comfort and elation mean for you; for example:
-   excited?
-   flushed?
-   happily pumping heart?
-   full of energy?
-   full of ideas?
-   full of enthusiasm?
-   feeling of harmony?

- feeling of fullness?
- feeling of calm?
- feeling of balance?

d) Notice what discomfort means for you; for example:
- a tight feeling in the pit of your stomach?
- a twitch in your neck?
- clenching your fist?
- thinking negative thoughts about the person you are with?
- sweating?
- blushing?
- feeling out of control?
- getting sick often?
- not feeling confident?
- feeling hyperactive?
- feeling of emptiness?
- grinding your teeth?

Note: Once you've recognized your symptoms, take the time to hone in on the problem (if there is one) and fix it.

Step 2: Listen with Empathy
"Seek First to Understand, then to be Understood."

- Stephen Covey,
The 7 Habits of Highly Effective People

Because communication is connected to so many variables (our own listening and speaking styles and others' styles), communication is both challenging and complex. Can you imagine a Bull who is wearing the Self-Protector listening mask while interacting with a non-assertive Elephant? A chatterbox Chimpanzee trying to get through to a Lion in a hurry who has his Attention Faker B listening mask on? Empathy *is* the critical ingredient to successful communication.

12 Strategies for Being an Empathic Communicator

1. Always listen to the words, the content, and the feelings.
2. Make an effort to understand others first, then let them get to know and understand you.
3. Always get feedback on issues that involve and affect the people you interact with, regardless of how they treat you.
4. State your position and walk a straight line. Keep walking a straight line regardless of what the other person does or doesn't do, says or doesn't say.
5. Be persuasive and be open to being persuaded.
6. Accept their concerns as your concerns.
7. Make sure you are prepared to hear what the other person has to say — even if you don't like it.
8. Attempt to move the situation forward.
9. Accept others' feelings.
10. You are responsible for resolving your feelings. Others are responsible for theirs.
11. Feelings vary. Some are short term, while others last a long time. Feelings aren't neat and they aren't simple. They do not necessarily happen at opportune times. So have realistic expectations when working with your own feelings and those of others.
12. Be a little vulnerable at the right time with the right people. Relationships are built on empathy and humility.

Follow-up Questions

➤ List three empathic communicators you've worked with. In each case, outline what is most appealing about their communications strategy. (You might like to think first about the Elephants, Chimpanzees and the Chameleons you know.)
➤ Do you consider yourself to be an empathic communicator?
➤ List your skills and behaviours that put you in this group.
➤ List three skills and behaviours you would like to improve on.

Step 3: Listen — but Don't Take on Other People's Feelings

I remember speaking with a colleague of mine, a lawyer, who is a Chameleon. One of her clients was having a really bad day. They spoke at length, and as a result of the conversation, she felt depleted of energy. The conversation stuck with her for a long time. She remembered it so well, she was able to aptly describe it a month later. It's important to show empathy when someone is having a rough time, but don't internalize someone else's feelings. You need to keep your energy for you and all the things you need to get done. You're not a sponge. Don't soak it up.

Step 4: Listen to meet Basic and Growth Needs

If we link quality listening to Abraham Maslow's (1968) "Self-Actualization Theory," we will be in a better position to see things from the other person's point of view. Maslow says we have five needs we have to satisfy. The first four are basic needs starting with the most basic:

1. physiological needs (food and water)
2. safety (shelter)
3. community (belonging)
4. self-esteem
5. growth.

It stands to reason that a need like hunger has to be satisfied first before we can fulfil our self-esteem need. All of our first four basic needs have to be satisfied before we can tackle need five — our need to grow. Maslow referred to our growth need as the need for justice, beauty, order and goodness. When we go on to satisfy these growth needs, we are said to be self-actualizing or actualizing our growth potential.

Let's look at Maslow through business eyes for just a moment. If a Human Resource manager is on deadline to meet the next payroll (basic need), will he be open to a discussion on a new voicemail enhancement (growth need)? If the sales manager's computer system, critical to her business, has just crashed (basic need), will she be able to listen to the promotional kick-off you have planned three months down the line (growth need)?

In "timing" your proposals, strategy meetings, important one-on-ones, charity drives, etc. make sure the basic needs of the people you are working with are taken into consideration. It will be impossible for them to truly listen to you unless their basic needs are met. On the personal side, it's the same. Make sure your basic needs are being met (example: your living space is safe, comfortable and gives you a sense of belonging) prior to embarking on an antique book collection (growth need). Your quest for intellectual fulfilment will not compensate for any imbalance in meeting your basic needs. What are you going to do with cranberry sauce if you don't have a turkey?

Follow-up Questions

➤ List three examples of situations where you have been able to really understand the other person's mindset. What enabled you to get into the other person's head?

➤ List three examples of situations where you were not able to understand the other person's mindset. What were the roadblocks to understanding? Had you been wearing a listening mask?

➤ List three examples of situations where someone was not able to understand your mindset. What were the roadblocks to understanding. Had you been wearing a listening mask? If so, why?

Step 5: Listen to Create a Win-Win

Based on the work of psychologist Carl Rogers, as communicators we build relationships with people by showing them they are understood and respected. If we try "to win" by defeating an opponent, both sides will lose in terms of long-term relationship building. If we look at the situation from the listener's mindset and show how our ideas are relevant to their needs, then there is an opportunity for true communication.

The Chinese pictogram for hearing is two ears and a heart. The empathic listener gets at the facts and the feelings. Empathics are experts at connecting the 18 inches between their heads and hearts and getting into another person's mindset. Much like a judge who takes all the circumstances into consideration before rendering a verdict, the empathic uses good judgement skills to make a double ruling, using head and heart, person by person, situation by situation.

Step 6: Listen to Show Respect

You know the old adage "Do unto others as you would have them do unto you." Well, it works. When you show interest in someone, and in what someone is saying to you, this is a sign of respect. And when you treat someone with respect, the likelihood of the person reciprocating such respect is good.

EXAMPLE

I'd like to share an example of a situation that happened to me. I've been taking my car into the same service centre for close to 10 years. During that time, I've built a good relationship with everyone whom I've had the opportunity to work with — from Larry, the head mechanic, to the car jockey. The solidarity that's been created is based on three operating principles:

a) A car is a mechanical device and things can and will go wrong.

   If you're in a bad mood because something's wrong with your car, don't take your anger out on the people who can help to fix the problem. It's not their fault, and these people can help.

b) It's up to me to understand the problem.

   I want to understand what my car problem is. As this isn't my field, I ask people to explain it to me. They share their knowledge and I listen and ask questions.

c) Be nice — it's the same price.

   I ask people how they're doing, if their families are well, we talk a little shop, etc. Everyone wants to feel comfortable and appreciated. Rudyard Kipling said, "Teach us to delight in the simple things." This is a key concept in relationship building, and is often neglected.

I was laughing hard at one of my friend's jokes on the telephone one Friday night and leaned back too far in my swivel chair. The chair's spring mechanism popped. I was left with four parts on the floor and a very frightened cat who had been prematurely ejected from my lap.

On the advice of another friend, I took the chair to a fix-it shop. After careful examination, the owner concluded that I needed a "spring compressor" to re-attach the spring, and that he didn't think he could do it. He suggested I go and see my mechanic. So, I did.

Larry laughed when I told him the story, triple-bolted the spring in 30 seconds (without even removing the chair from the car) and I was gone — and very happy. And Larry was delighted he could help.

Step 7: Listen to Gain Insight and Understanding

Following are some techniques to help gain insight and understanding in all interactions.

a) Clarify the facts
- to get additional facts and ideas
- to understand the speaker's expectations
- to help the person explore all sides of an issue

Sample questions:
- Can you clarify this?
- Can you give me some more information about?
- Do you mean...?
- Is this the problem as you see it?
- I'd like to find out some more about ...?
- Exactly, how would you like to proceed from here?
- May I ask you a couple of questions about ...?

b) Clarify the feelings
- to show that you understand how they feel about what they are saying
- to help them evaluate and moderate their own feelings as expressed by someone else

Sample questions:
- Do you feel that you didn't get a fair shake?
- Are you ... angry, frustrated, disappointed, hurt, happy, sad, intimidated, surprised, scared, nervous, etc.?
- Do you feel that no one is interested in your opinion?

Note: Chimpanzees, Elephants and Chameleons are competent in helping to clarify feelings, so you might like to watch them on the job.

c) Restate
- to check our interpretation with the other person
- to confirm expectations on both sides and alleviate any future disappointments and hurts
- to show you are listening and have understood

- to make the speaker feel listened to and understood
- to encourage the speaker to look at other aspects of the issue and to discuss it with you

Sample questions:
- As I understand it then your idea is to ...
- So, this is what you have decided to do and the reasons are ...
- If I understood you correctly, your plan is to ...
- I'd like to review what you said to make sure I understand ...

Other ways to show understanding:
- silence (this one can work both ways)
- sounds of acknowledgement (uh uh, mmmmm, uh-huh)
- exclamations (oh! yes! gee!)
- body movements (head nodding)
- facial movements (eyebrows raised, smiling)
- asking questions
- demonstrating keen attention (focused eye contact)
- posture (interested)

d) Be neutral
- to convey that you are interested and listening
- to encourage the person to continue talking
- to get all the needed information
- to make the person feel secure that you are not judging him/her

Examples:
- I see.
- Uh-huh.
- That's interesting.
- I understand.
- Thank you for sharing that with me.
- Is there anything else you want to share with me?
- Okay.
- Please continue.
- I'd like to hear more.

What does staying neutral look like?
Very few people can really listen and remain neutral. For example,
Bill is recounting for Stan what happened at the last team meeting.

> Bill: Boy Stan, did you miss a beaut!
>
> Stan: What do you mean?
>
> Bill: Ray tore a strip off John.
>
> Stan: Really? (Stan's voice has a tone of surprise and concern.
> He has no information yet but is beginning to get a little wor-
> ried. John is one of Stan's peers, and he likes him.)
>
> Bill: Well, I guess I'm exaggerating a bit. Ray went over our
> numbers, and looked straight at John when he said some peo-
> ple haven't pulled their weight this quarter.
>
> Stan (concerned): Did Ray speak to John after?
>
> Bill: No, but you could tell Ray wasn't pleased.

1. Was Bill neutral in how he read the situation with Ray and John?
2. Is there anything in the information that points to Ray being disappointed with John?
3. Was Ray actually zeroing in on John? Why might Bill have interpreted it this way?
4. Was Stan neutral when he was listening to Bill?
5. What kind of a listener is Stan?

e) Summarize
– to bring all of the discussion into focus
– to act as a springboard for more discussion on a new aspect of
  the issue

Sample statements:
– These are the key ideas you have expressed ...
– If I understand how you feel about the situation ...
– So, if I can bring together everything you've shared with me ...

f) Prepare
– to describe how you hope the person will respond to your message before you send it
– to "cushion the blow" in cases where the news may be difficult,
  and you want to prepare the listener for the shock, surprise, disappointment, etc.

Sample statements:
- This is a difficult topic for me and I am concerned that you will have a bad reaction. Please sit down.
- This is hard for me to talk about and I don't want to hurt you.
- I hope we can talk this through together.
- I have some bad news. I want you to know that I'm here for you if you need me.
- You're not going to like this, but ...

g) Nobody likes to be "should upon"

"Advice is seldom welcome, and those who need it most like it least."

- Samuel Johnson

Share your opinions with others, invite participation and give advice when asked. In an effort to be helpful, the Lion, the Peacock and the Bull (see Bernard and Nicole in Chapter 6) often "tell" people what to do (whether they're asked for advice or not), and this can be misinterpreted. Expressions in giving feedback and advice that need to be avoided are:

- you should
- you ought to
- you must
- don't you need to?
- you need to
- you have to
- why don't/didn't you?

These finger-pointing expressions may encourage the listener to put on either the Selective or Self-Protector listening mask. Focus on asking for what you want and need, and do not tell the other person what would work best for him/her.

In conversation, I remember telling a friend a couple of weeks after I'd gotten my cat that I had to take her in to be spayed. I was greeted with a didactic yet well-intentioned, "You should really breed her." My response was an equally well-intentioned, "But, I don't *want* to be a breeder."

In this case, to encourage me to understand her mindset, my friend could have used expressions like "I would love to have a cat

like that so I could breed her," or "Have you ever thought of breed-
ing your cat?" Other useful expressions:

- I need ...
- I must have ...
- I want ...
- I would find it helpful if...
- What I am expecting is ...
- I'd appreciate it if we could ...
- I like/I don't like ...
- What I'd like to see is ...

h) Appreciate and value the message

As humans, we tend to label and categorize things to help us better understand them. By putting things in "quick categories," we
can see things more clearly. Quick categories follow the pattern of
typical listener reactions such as:

- right/wrong
- good/bad
- correct/incorrect
- okay/not okay
- doable/not doable
- yes/no

The potential danger in doing this is that sometimes we label the
person with the behaviour or situation. We need to consistently
demonstrate in dialogue that (i) we're not judging the speaker, and
(ii) that we find value in the message (even if we disagree).
    To show value you can:

1. Pick up on the parts of the discussion that you can naturally add
   to and build on. Phrases like "yes and," "absolutely and," and "I
   appreciate where you're coming from" will move you in this
   direction.
2. Tell the other person what you found useful about the comment, or what you learned from the discussion.
3. Let the other stuff go unless there is a productive purpose in
   pursuing it.

Step 8: Performing a Productive Listening Autopsy (PLA)

When there has been a miscommunication, and there exists a combination of bad feelings, unfinished work, frustrated peers and the like, it's useful to perform a listening autopsy and prepare an action plan.

Exercise

Retrace your part in the conversation. Note what you said, what you meant, the results of the conversation in terms of facts and feelings, and where you think the miscommunication occurred.

Action Plan

Once you are comfortable with your analysis, call the other party involved and ask him/her if you can talk things through. A number of message mediums are at your disposal here. Focus on the other person's comfort level. Always ask the other person what works best for him/her: in person (either in or out of the office), by phone (some people are highly adept on the phone while others need the visual to communicate), letter, fax or E-mail based on situation and distance.

Remember! Listening regulates the heartbeat of a relationship.

Communication Skill Set 3: Getting and Giving Feedback

"I see people getting hurt and disappointed all the time, and sometimes for a long time when they internalize feedback as negative. However, if you're confident in who you are and what you do, then you welcome feedback and learn from it."

- Walter Fox, *President, Hitachi Construction Machinery Canada Ltd.*

Feedback is generally a combination of facts and feelings, and there is a high risk for people to become disgruntled based on both the content message and the relationship message. In giving feedback, we need to stress the value for the person's growth and not sound judgemental and critical. In getting feedback, we need to take what's valuable for us and run with it — no matter who delivers the message or in what form. But based on our 13 Potential Crash Sites, it's easy to take things personally. And when someone is giving feedback in a negative way, it can lesson the impact of the content message and cause a rift in the relationship.

In a *For Better or For Worse* comic strip by Lynn Johnson, Michael's mother is giving him some feedback at the breakfast table. She tells him his table manners are absolutely disgusting. She orders him to sit up straight, to use the cutlery correctly and to chew with his mouth closed. She goes on to tell him how sloppy he's become: that his hair's too long, his clothes too wrinkled and that if she were a girl going out with him that she'd be appalled and would probably never go out with him again. As he grabs a cookie on his way out, she asks if he is listening to her. He mumbles "sure." As he quickly heads for the door head down, she says that she hopes he learned something from all that, and Michael answers a despairing "yeah." As Michael quietly exits the house we hear him finishing his thought: "Never date anyone like my mother."

Here, the mother's well-intentioned advice may have a number of possible outcomes.

1. Michael will most likely ignore all of the repair work she's suggested because of the manner in which she gave it to him. In the end, a detriment to Michael and a waste of his mother's effort.
2. Michael has now developed a mindset about his mother and perhaps other people, specifically other women like her which may cause him angst in his personal and professional relationships.
3. The relationship between Michael and his mother may change as a result of this incident, especially if this happens on a continual basis.
4. A vulnerable teenager, Michael may let his mother's opinions affect his self-image. As we discussed in Chapter 2, it's easy to take on other people's opinions as facts when you're not clear on the difference.

Feedback and Power

Harry, a new sales representative, is giving his first presentation to the management team, and he asks his new colleague Frank to sit-in on the presentation and give him some feedback. From the nods of interest, questions and applause, Harry has concluded things have gone well. He's pleased and looking forward to his conversation with Frank to get further input.

EXAMPLE

Harry: So, what did you think?

Frank (sarcastic): Well, your overheads were *very unprofessional*. They look like something a teacher would use. You'll *never* make a half-a-million-dollar sale with those.

Harry (disappointed): Yeah, I guess they could use a makeover.

Frank: Also, I really wouldn't feel comfortable asking you to substitute for me with any of my clients.

Harry: Why not?

Frank: Well, you've got a lot more content than me and you'd make me look bad.

ANALYSIS

Feeling threatened, Frank is unable to give Harry the credit he deserves for his solid presentation. The good news is, Harry found out four valuable things:

1) exactly what he could expect from Frank in the future

2) that his overheads could look better so he immediately made plans to get them redone

3) that Frank is biased towards teachers (later Harry finds out that Frank is insecure around anyone who went to university — he didn't)

4) more confirmation of just how talented Harry really is.

Feedback and Solidarity

"Whenever I've had a situation where I've had to reprimand someone, I tell them not to take it personally. But sometimes they do because they associate it with failure. When people gave/give me feedback, I always did/do two things: First, I look at the source and, if I don't respect the person, I just turn off, and second, if I value the person and the feedback, I look at it as an opportunity to grow. And yes sometimes, it might hurt a little. But the important part is that I get better at how to do something."

- Nancy Adamo, *President, Hockley Valley Inn*

I remember the first time I facilitated my day-long business writing workshop at Ryerson Polytechnic University in Toronto several years ago. I was nervous and had talked a lot. At the end of the day, a secretary attending the workshop shyly came up to tell me that she had found it hard to concentrate on the grammar exercises as I had kept talking during much of the time allotted to do the assignment. I was surprised and very grateful. I wouldn't have known this had she not told me, and would not have been able to easily correct this problem in my next workshop.

Remember! When you get feedback, no matter in what form it's in or the "status" of the giver, if there's value in it for you, use it.

Communication Skill Set 4: Dealing with Fear

To deal with fear, we need to separate ourselves from the issue; in other words, not to take it personally. Following is a personal account from a middle manager in a mid-size Canadian organization who was able to conquer her fears and move herself and the situation forward:

> "I worked for an organization once where the president was always in a hurry and didn't trust anyone to get anything done. But instead of taking it personally, I grew because I learned how not to react and not to run from her putdowns. I built enough courage to deal with my fears and to deal with her. Actually, being dumped on was a badge of honour — a sign that I was part of her inner sanctum, that she trusted me enough to dump on me. Once when I needed her input to complete an assignment, she didn't come through, and blamed me for coming to her too late to get the information. She followed up with a nasty voice mail from her car which I couldn't afford to take personally. Ten minutes later, she called back and apologized on voice mail. In the end, she turned out to be one of my best references."
>
> - A middle manager, *Canadian corporation,*
> *in correspondence with the author*

Fear is linked to personal and professional change. We fear things and people we don't know and don't understand. To move forward, it means you have to purposefully decide to leave something behind, to let something go.

EXAMPLE

Tremblay Corp. is in the midst of a major change initiative, and the team captain is having a difficult time getting his staff to commit to the new way of doing things. The staff are very happy with the way they've been doing things for the last 20 years.

Team Captain (with empathy): I know this is a big switch from how you are used to working on the floor.

Team Supervisor (concerned): It sure is. I'm used to running things, not to checking in with someone all the time.

Team Captain (with enthusiasm): Well, this system will help you to get better at several things. First, you won't be accountable for the whole shop floor, alone. Your teammate will share the responsibility. When there's a problem, you'll have a partner to work through things with. Second, it will help you to better monitor where the problems are, how often they occur and at what times of the day. This will help you be proactive in solving problems. Third, it will free you up to focus on using all your experience to help the company move forward. *We need you now more than ever, Peter.* We're going through a major shift in thinking and doing. And we need folks like you on board who are good at both these things.

Team Supervisor (sincerely, feeling a little more comfortable): I appreciate your encouragement. Let's give it a shot and see how it goes.

Team Captain (smiles): Fine.

ANALYSIS

The team captain respects his supervisor and wants his commitment not just compliance to the new process. He strategically points out the benefits of the new process to the supervisor, and in so doing gives him credit for his work and his knowledge.

His style is upbeat, energetic and committed, and is the perfect foil to erase the supervisor's discomfort and scepticism.

Remember! When you move through the fear, you gain feelings of competency and self-esteem.

Communication Skill Set 5: Being Honest

By being honest with others you increase the odds of building solid, long-lasting relationships. Sometimes, the truth does hurt, but ultimately honesty is the best policy for relationship building.

The 12-year chronic buildup
I received a letter from a friend that aptly described how and why relationships erode. She had an abrupt and unpleasant ending to a 12-year friendship:

"I guess it really comes down to our inability to be honest with one another. Someone does or says something that really bugs you but you don't want to say anything for fear of hurting their feelings. So, you store up all these things over a period of years, and one day you get into a fight about something really stupid. You never end up discussing the issues behind the something stupid, though. And the friendship disintegrates."

Following is another example of how lack of honesty leads to resentment and eventually loss of the relationship:

"Deep down I've always believed that if you really tell someone straight what's bothering you about the relationship, it's doomed. I've always been so afraid of hurting people's feelings or being confrontational, that I allow the resentment to build until I finally just turn my back on the relationship once and for all. I've had this problem in work relationships — not being able to speak frankly to my boss about things that bother me about the job or the company. So, I just quit and find another job. I guess it's a fear of being hurt myself."

- A corporate public relations manager,
in discussion with the author

Remember! It's important to be honest and get at the things that bug you at the time before they have a chance to grow and fester.

Communication Skill Set 6: Working with Anger

Where does anger come from?

– when our wants and needs are not met
– when we are frustrated because of competing needs
– when we bury feelings of frustration, hurt and disappointed and they are released as anger
– when we have a buildup of past grudges and resentments

What do angry people want?

An opportunity:
– to vent and get their anger out
– to right a wrong and feel satisfied and justified
– to clear the air and/or fix the problem
– to feel empathy, get sympathy or both
– to get an apology.

When someone is angry and you are not the cause of the anger, you need to interpret the situation accurately and not take it personally. Let's look at the following dialogue.

EXAMPLE

Wendy: I am so angry. Brian asked for my help in purchasing a new copier when he was pressed for time, and now he's blaming me because the motor died. I'm not responsible for a mechanical device that stops working. He doesn't appreciate me or the help I gave him at all.

Candice: Sounds like he was really upset and lost it.

Wendy: Yeah, but it's not fair to take it out on me.

Candice: You're right. Maybe you need to talk to him about it.

Wendy: What can I say? He blames me and I'm angry and hurt.

ANALYSIS

It sounds like Brian got caught up in the problem and is in a rut. Wendy has taken this personally, and naturally so as she was kind and acted in good faith. Wendy will have to make a decision to (i) reframe it and not take it personally and then let it go, or (ii) confront Brian on the situation once her hurt has subsided and they can discuss it productively.

When a person is angry, how do you not take it personally and help him to cope? Here are some ways:

- acknowledge their feelings
- fact find (get to the true source of the anger)
- use all of the listening techniques to make sure you understand where the other person is coming from (e.g., clarify, paraphrase, etc.)
- show empathy
- state your position
- ask if your help, advice, etc. is wanted
- focus on the problem
- buy time as needed
- don't reinforce negative behaviour
- watch very carefully — often their bodies will tell the tale.

If you're angry, don't stuff it — huff it!
If you're angry and you've decided it's worth it, talk it through with the person who you've got the problem with. Listen to your anger and let it direct you in fixing the problem. Don't jog, eat, listen to music, scream at your mate, cry or analyze the situation 16 times. Don't avoid the anger and go to the source provided this is possible. This is the best way to clear the anger. Permanently. Then after you've cleared the air, clear your gut. You'll feel much better and the anger will never have a chance to build into resentment. You're important and so are your feelings, and camouflaging your anger will only hurt you and in no way diminish the problem.

or

Understand your own or someone's calculated anger for what it is, and work with it to your advantage. Like an experienced swimmer, let the power of the current propel you. In this case, let the anger guide you upstream — to act productively. It's amazing what tasks you can accomplish when you are angry. Clean up your office. Plant a garden. Finish a long-overdue report. Go for a swim. Conduct a great media interview.

> "We put our egos on the line. If we take anger personally, then we take it as a personal rejection. If we personalize it, then we're setting ourselves up for a fall. With media, for example, if they get angry, it's usually a calculated anger because they want to get you going and to get a good story. When you realize that, then you can be more objective."
>
> - Rick Winston, *Media Relations Director, SunLife of Canada*

Remember! The healthiest response to anger in general is to discuss the incident with the person who provoked the anger. Work it through and move on — and don't carry it around inside. To quote Bonnie Bickel, the president of B.B. Bargoons, "Confront it straight on."

Communication Skill Set 7: Creating Positive Confrontation

"A friend is a person who I can talk to and talk difficult things through with. A friend is not a person who avoids communication with me."

> - Bob Dameron, *Vice-President, Sales, Financial Services Industry*

Most negotiation strategies and self-help tools look at confrontation as some kind of last resort. A dirty word. When all else has failed, confront. Why? A straightforward honest and caring confrontation can quickly clear the air and allow the relationship to move forward. Confrontations can take many forms: a short, quick chat, a longer talk if needed. They are an opportunity to set things straight, make things right. In confrontation, no one is out to kill a fly with a machine gun. Just do what's needed to fix the problem.

First, you have to decide:

1.   What do I stand to gain?
2.   What do I stand to lose?
3.   Is it worth it?

Remember! If you choose not to confront, make your choice from strength not fear. At times, the wisest decision is to not confront and to walk away.

Communication Skill Set 8: Making Decisions

If you can't make a decision because you're beat, worried, not feeling well, preoccupied, starving (a relative term in North America, of course), whatever the case may be, say so. And the people you work with will appreciate your candour and humility. Then commit to a time when you can give your best to the situation and the people involved and follow through.

However, if indecision-itis persists, you've got to do something. Here are some steps to help you. As we've seen, this is a particular growth area for the Elephant and the Chimpanzee.

The Decision-making Process

Step 1:   Review the facts.
Step 2:   Go over alternate solutions.
Step 3:   Choose the best one. Even if it means cutting your losses.
Step 4:   Act on it.
Step 5:   Move on. Don't second-guess yourself. You've done your homework. If it doesn't work, you'll shift course and try again. That's how we learn.

If you don't make a decision, nothing might happen — for a long time. And you may be unwittingly grinding down productivity and morale. If the wrong person's in a spot, it affects everyone. Don't plug a hole with chewing gum. But let there be a hole until it's properly filled.

Remember! Avoiding making decisions leads to increased procrastination and eventually tears at your self-esteem, and in many cases the self-esteem of others involved. Why procrastinate at being happy? Make your decision and follow through.

Communication Skill Set 9: Gaining Closure

"I wrote a letter to Emily not too long ago. In it, I apologized to her for my behaviour and especially for my gaffes as a communicator. I failed myself and I failed her. I told her I think good thoughts about her and wish her all the best. While it's too late for us, and I really don't want her back in my life (I don't like her energy), I can now (two years later) get past the hurt and anger and take responsibility for my part in the break. Now, I have a sense of peace and closure.

- A middle manager,
in correspondence with the author

Gaining closure allows you to put a person/situation in perspective and move on. No one likes to have unfinished business in their lives. It can take you away from the business of living in the "now." Here are some options that may work for you.

Option 1: Write the letter for yourself and don't mail it, as was the case in the Emily letter above.

Option 2: Write the letter for yourself and for the other person. If you feel so much better, imagine how the other person might feel. What do you lose by being generous and mailing it? You might just make someone else's day.

Option 3: Gain closure by phone.

Option 4: Gain closure in a face-to-face meeting.

Remember! Closure is a gift you give yourself.

Communication Skill Building Set 10: Letting Go

"Why does the eagle fly so high? Because it takes itself so lightly."

- Anon.

If you've been hurt and disappointed because of a miscommunication, don't hang onto it. Ask yourself: how do I want to feel? Do I want to carry around this baggage? What do I gain?

Once you've earnestly given it your best shot to clear up the miscommunication, take credit for your effort, stop suffering, and enjoy the tremendous relief it brings. And the time it gives you to pursue the things you want to do — that give you fulfilment and pleasure.

In one of my recent workshops, a participant described a public relations campaign she had run for a client, where the client's expectations had not been fully met. The client acted as if a tragedy had occurred, as if the problem were the end of the world. As a result of the client losing perspective (perhaps not having enough to start with), the consultant in charge beat up on herself quite badly. When we discussed the fact that she was too hard on herself, she replied, "That's true, but there is a natural grieving process involved." Once you analyze what went wrong and what you will do differently the next time, it's time to let go. Letting go is part of accepting that you're human and that it's human to make mistakes. The important thing is to learn from them.

―――

Remember! Building your communication strengths requires perseverance — a combination of persistence and patience. Keep the end in mind, feel comfortable with the tools you are using, and practise.

So Strategy 7 of the *How Not To Take It Personally Action Plan* is to Tune into Your 10 Communication Skills and Build on Them.

Let's review the four steps to increase our knowledge and apply them.

1. Build on the things you're good at to get even better.
2. Practice the things you're not so good at.
3. Be fair to yourself and others.
4. Accept the fact that you're not perfect, but that you certainly are "enough."[17]

CHAPTER 8

THE WORLD IS FULL OF CHALLENGING PERSONALITIES

"The reasonable man adapts himself to the world. The unreasonable one persists in trying to adapt the world to himself. Therefore all progress depends on the unreasonable man."

- George Bernard Shaw

Strategy 8:   *Recognize and Interact Productively with the Six Challenging Personalities*

THE SIX CHALLENGING PERSONALITIES

We've been working hard throughout the book to build our communication strengths. And we need them now (more than ever) to be successful in dealing with the Six Challenging Personalities. In this chapter we will get to know the Six Challenging Personalities, all of their sub-types, how to aim your rifle appropriately at each and to hit the target.

Challenging personalities span the cross-section of people you know in age, shape, culture, gender, profession, and listening and speaking styles. You may run into an Elephant who holds a grudge, or a Lion who likes to whine, a controlling Chimpanzee, a prickly Peacock, or a Bull who is an ardent do-it-all.

You may find that people who are prone to wearing the Self-Protector listening mask may be Pricklies, that Selective listeners may be Manipulators, and that Attention Fakers are also sometimes Pleasers. To quote Forrest Gump's mother in the 1994 Academy

Award-winning film *Forrest Gump,* "Life is like a box of chocolates. You never know what you're going to get."[18] So, be prepared.

There are six types of challenging personalities:

1. The Manipulators — act in certain ways to gain power and control over people and situations
2. The Experts — think they're really hot stuff at everything they do and that they know everything
3. The Reactors — react immediately with feelings (emotion) rather than responding (facts and feelings)
4. The Complainers — love to gripe and have you listen to and feel sorry for them
5. The Pleasers — "do" non-stop for others and conform to others' opinions to be liked and accepted
6. The Pricklies — appear prickly on the outside to protect themselves because they are mushy on the inside

Your knowledge of the six listening masks, the features and tools of spoken English, the six speaking styles and the six types of challenging personalities will help you turn every interaction into a potential success. Of course, the first success strategy as always is building your self-awareness. Do you have a challenging personality? Do you ever whine? Hold a grudge? Try to be perfect and drive every one else nuts? And what happens when two people with challenging personalities get together?

I started working at Yorkdale, Toronto and Canada's first indoor shopping mall when I was 15. I could never get over the fact that if there were six people at Simpson's jewellery counter, inevitably it was the hard-core consumer, furious and ranting because our sale was over, who came to me for help. Or the teenager who had bought a necklace for someone and worn it 10 times before deciding she didn't really like it and wanted to return it, without a bill! For years, I wondered why. Why me? Why do I always get them? I always felt burdened and put upon. And just frustrated.

Then, one day it hit me. I was on a mission. A quest. It was actually a good thing that all the problem cases came my way. That I was being challenged — challenged to adapt my communication style to make any situation workable. Once I was able to see these challenging personalities as a fruitful source for my own growth in communication, both personally and professionally, I started casting my fishing rod into troubled waters hoping for a nibble. And I got hooked.

In her wonderful book *Dealing with Difficult Men*, author Dr. Judith Segal recommends we put the difficult man on a slide and have a good look at him under a microscope. She also recommends we then look at ourselves under the same microscope with a focus on our own behaviour.[19] I thought this was smart advice, and I'd like to adopt this philosophy in our gender neutral discussion of the six types of challenging personalities.

Are You a Magnet for Challenging Personalities?

To kick off your foray into the world of challenging personalities, think about the people in your life both at home and at work. Are you a magnet for people with challenging personalities? And are you one of them yourself?

The Challenging Personality Magnet Quiz

1. Do challenging personalities you know:

➤ try to scare you with their anger?

➤ plan a well-calculated revenge?

➤ scream, swear or cry to get their way?

➤ play the dramatist?

➤ latch onto you and never let go?

2. Do challenging personalities you know:

➤ think you're stupid?

➤ think they're perfect?

➤ blow themselves out of proportion?

➤ refuse to revise their opinion in light of new data?

➤ judge you by their standards?

3. Do challenging personalities you know:

➤ act like victims?

➤ hold grudges forever (or close to forever?)

➤ explode on certain cues?

➤ display jealousy?

➤ blame others for their problems?

4. Do challenging personalities you know:

➤ love to whine?

➤ see the glass as half empty?

➤ feel they should have everything "coming to them"?

➤ commit to a cause beyond the exclusion of all else?

➤ take but don't give half as much?

5. Do challenging personalities you know:

➤ fudge the truth to spare your feelings?

➤ conform to everyone's wishes?

➤ say "yes" all the time?

➤ try to be superhuman?

➤ wipe themselves out trying to please everyone?

6. Do challenging personalities you know:

➤ show kindness in little ways?

➤ keep you at bay but secretly want you around?

➤ have a tough exterior?

➤ worry about you but don't talk about it?

➤ hide how much they care but are always there if you need them?

Keep your answers handy. As we work through the six challenging personalities, you will be able to track which types you seem to most attract. And perhaps discover some things about yourself in the process. Could you be one of the challenging personalities?

Remember! Water seeks its own level.[20]

1. The Manipulators

Manipulators can appear irrational in their outbursts, but actually use their anger, histrionics, guilt-inducing tactics and vengefulness to try to control and manipulate the other person and situation.

The Manipulators fall into four groups:

i)   The Snipers

ii) The Stormin' Normans

iii) The Dramatists

iv) The Leeches

i) The Snipers

"That which does not kill me makes me stronger."

- Fredrich Nietzsche

Snipers are out for revenge and they hit you outright, or from behind verbally, or in action either when you are aware of the attack or when you least expect it. Although snipers do miss, good ones strategically aim to hit one of five specific locations:

➤ A shot in the foot: If you're not 100 percent supportive of the department's stand on this issue, you're out.

➤ A shot in the knee: You're friendly with a colleague, and have spoken with her several times. She invites you to a seminar she is hosting. You can't make it. In a subsequent conversation, she invites you to the next workshop, and again for personal and professional reasons you decline. She tells you of your obligation to attend her workshop. When you decline, she ends the association.

➤ A shot in the gut: Friend A asks Friend B to pick her up at the airport. The flight is one hour early. Friend A does not contact friend B, and unknowingly friend B, who is on time, stays at the airport and waits an extra hour. Friend B returns home, calls friend A, finds out about the early arrival and Friend A says "I'm just sorry I had to *spend $40 on cab fare!*"

➤ A shot in the head: A retailer in the desktop publishing business puts herself out for a client, and does a lot of extra work to help him prepare for an important presentation. When he gets to the meeting, he tells everyone the desktop publisher was too expensive.

➤ A shot in the heart: Choosing the person's most vulnerable spot and aiming for a direct hit (someone has confided a deep, dark secret and you use it against the person to hurt him).

EXAMPLE

Following is a true sniper story where the sniper succeeded in shooting his victim in the knees, but ended up shooting himself in the head!

Three acquaintances — Trevor, Martin and Jack — went on a camping trip. The drive was eight hours each way and it was agreed in advance that each person would contribute $100 toward gas and other expenses. Trevor drove his car. Whenever Trevor stopped to fill up, Jack conveniently could never find his wallet. Trevor became increasingly more frustrated throughout the trip. Finally, when Trevor dropped Jack off at his door, he demanded his $100. Again, Jack couldn't find his wallet. In frustration and out of spite, the sniper, Trevor drove off with Jack's $70 sleeping bag, — a strategy that achieved nothing. Trevor never saw any of his money and got stuck with a sleeping bag he didn't want or need!

ii) The Stormin' Normans

The Stormin' Normans use what appears to be irrational behaviour, generally an outburst of anger, to control others and the outcome of a situation. Remember! A Norman, or Sophie in the following example, can only take control if you let them.

EXAMPLE

Three business associates are lunching. Jean is a partner in an accounting firm and Sophie is an accountant at the same firm. Mickey works in high-tech communications. Jean and Mickey go for the lunch buffet; Sophie orders from the menu. For dessert, Sophie orders from the menu plus asks Jean to bring her a second dessert from the buffet table. When the waiter brings the cheque, he carefully touches Sophie's shoulder and quietly says, "I didn't charge you for that extra dessert." Sophie acts mortally wounded, leers at him and angrily barks, "No tip for him," and repeats this again when the waiter brings Jean the bill.

Jean and Mickey look at each other and are extremely uncomfortable. Jean has the bill and is feeling uncertain about what to do. The waiter had been superb over their luxurious two hour lunch. Mickey suggests they call the waiter over. Jean is relieved, and asks that Mickey handle it as she has no idea how to.

Mickey (politely): Excuse me (Mickey gets the waiter's attention). Hi. May I ask you something?

Waiter (professionally): Of course.

Mickey (pleasantly): When you gave us the bill, you told my friend that you didn't charge her for the extra dessert. Would you please explain?

Waiter (pleasantly): That's right. Dessert from the buffet table costs an extra $3.95. But I spoke with my manager and I told him I didn't want to charge you for it. He said it was okay. I've been here for 12 years, and I could lose my job if I don't report things like this. I apologize if I hurt anyone's feelings.

Mickey (sincerely): Thank you very much.

Mickey to Sophie (happily): Well, how do you feel now?

Sophie (angrily): Well, I accept his apology *but I don't accept his explanation.*

(Mickey and Jean look at each other in shock.)

Mickey to Jean: How do you feel?

Jean: I think he was perfectly right.

(Mickey smiles at Jean.)

Unable to accept responsibility for her error, Sophie tries to make Mickey feel uncomfortable and detract from the way Mickey handled the situation.

Sophie to Mickey (nastily): You know, you *intimidated* him.

Mickey (strategically): Really, Jean do you think so?

Jean (sincerely): No. I think you handled it perfectly. Thanks.

(The waiter got his tip!)

ANALYSIS
Mickey and Jean wanted to make sure the waiter, who had done a good job and who was professional and considerate in how he handled the problem, was fairly treated. Sophie refused to accept responsibility for cheating on the dessert table and instead accused the waiter of both offending her and of not doing a good job. Neither was true. In addition, Sophie then attempted to make Mickey feel uncomfortable for trying to fix the problem. Mickey did not intimidate the waiter; rather, Sophie was intimidated by Mickey's actions to clear the waiter and secure the tip as it made her look bad.

iii) The Dramatists
Dramatists use various forms of histrionics to captivate their audience and lure them into giving them what they want. In the following example, Mimi is playing the role of wounded friend to cover up her own lack of initiative and caring.

EXAMPLE

Mimi (acting offended): Your mother's been sick for two months. Why haven't you called me to tell me how she is doing?

Susan (earnestly and put off): I've been running back and forth to the hospital. Don't you have a phone?

Mimi (melodramatically): *It's your job* to call me and let me know how she's doing.

Susan: I really don't have any more time for this. (Susan hangs up and Mimi calls back.)

Mimi (quietly): I just wanted to tell you it would have been really hard to get in touch with me. We were in Portugal for five weeks.

Susan (audible sigh of exasperation).

ANALYSIS

Mimi, the dramatist, has done everything possible to make herself look like the injured party, then she finally owns up.

iv) The Leeches

Leeches cling to others to get whatever they can. And they render no service in return. Human parasites, they don't stop clinging unless you cut the vine. Great guilt inducers, they try to obligate you to help them. They have no shame, are never embarrassed and just keep asking.

EXAMPLE

Madeleine and Lenny have consistently helped their special project teammates, Bill and Shirley, in turning out a quality product since their team came together three months prior. Bill and Shirley now turn to Madeleine and Lenny for help at every opportunity, whether related to the project or not, and the latter are beginning to feel put upon.

ANALYSIS

Madeleine and Frank did their best to build a strong team by walking the talk and helping their teammates as needed. However, Bill and Shirley "felt free" to keep asking for help on too regular a basis. When someone doesn't know how to set self-limits, he can easily become a leech.

How to Deal with the Manipulators

- don't try to change them; see them and accept them for who they are
- listen briefly, and carefully and watch for the manipulation
- play the game if it's good for you and go after what you want
- enjoy the ride (even the bumps)
- don't take it personally

If you're a Manipulator:

- look at your behaviour: how do you feel about what you are doing?
- look at the results of your behaviour: is this what you want?
- think about making a change in your behaviour if it's worth the trade and the effort

Follow-up Questions

➤ List one situation where the Manipulator came around and saw your point of view.

➤ List one situation where you refused to play the Manipulator's game and things worked out well.

➤ List one situation where you were the Manipulator. Was this a conscious decision? If so, why?

2. The Experts

The Experts think they are pros at everything, that they are always right, that their opinions have more value than anyone else's. In general that they are simply the best. So, you must be second best and know a helluva lot less than they do.

The Experts fall into four groups:

i) The Inflexibles
ii) The Perfectionists
iii) The Know-It-Alls
iv) The Exaggerators

i) The Inflexibles

The Inflexible see things from only one perspective — their own. They won't budge and will fight to the death to get you to come around and see their point of view or at least have theirs accepted as correct.

EXAMPLE

Henry came home from a meeting at midnight. He checked on his wife and children who were asleep, turned the computer on in his home office and set to work. The computer woke his wife, Caroline, sleeping in the next room.

Caroline was furious that her husband had come home so late and told him he should be finishing his work at some other time of day. Henry refused to apologize for not shutting the office door and for waking her (she had to get up at 6:00 a.m. the next morning for work), insisted he was on deadline and had to work. Henry refused to see Caroline's perspective and vice versa. They ended up fighting all night and nothing was resolved. Caroline accused Henry of having Henryvision: being only able to see things from his viewpoint. In reality, both were totally self-absorbed.

ANALYSIS

Here two inflexibles, both angry and self-righteous, and undoubtedly with valid reasons for their feelings, fight to the end with conviction. But since no one will budge an inch, acknowledge the other's perspective, make a compromise and extend an apology, the situation remained stalemated.

ii) The Perfectionists

"Not Good Enough" is the motto of the perfectionist. Have you ever met anyone who washes fruit once on the way into the refrigerator and again on the way out (the same fruit, that is). Who insists the dishes be done immediately after dinner? Who won't rest until their living space is in perfect order? Whose closets look like they were designed for a movie set?

Perfectionists can be awesome to deal with. They have unrealistic expectations (there's no such thing as perfect) and, as a result, set impossible standards for themselves and can be equally hard (or harder) on others. One perfectionist I know evaluated whether his best friend's partner was "good enough" based on her reading repertoire. The funny part is that the perfectionist who was doing the evaluating wasn't well read at all.

iii) The Know-It-Alls

"It infuriates me to be wrong when I know I'm right."

- Molière

The Know-It-All appears to think he or she is an expert on or at everything, even when they haven't got a clue. If you golf, so do they, and better than you do. If you're a dental hygienist, the know-it-all (who's totally out of his field) will be keen to share his opinions and advice with you. Some Know-It-Alls also think you know nothing and can appear condescending and rude.

EXAMPLE

Three managers are crowded around the photocopier that isn't working. They are struggling to figure out what's wrong, but won't ask for help. When a colleague does come to the rescue, they learn that the copier was out of paper. They didn't know how to read the error message, but refused to ask for help.

In a self-service copy outlet:

Customer: I'd like to use the copier please.

Manager: Let me show you how to use it.

Customer (angry): I *know* how to use the copy machine.

(Manager watches from the corner of her eye and the customer is botching it up big time.)

Manager: Perhaps I should show you how to use it. It's *cheaper* that way.

Customer: How much do I owe you?

Manager: It's ten cents a copy — *even the ones you wrecked.*

ANALYSIS

In both examples, the copy experts didn't believe they could possibly be in need of help of any kind, and the manager made her point.

iv) The Exaggerators

The Exaggerator likes to stretch things a little. Or a lot. In a *For Better or Worse* comic strip, the young Mr. Patterson is looking for work. He says he has experience as a short-order cook. We learn he worked as a hotdog vendor. He says he's a winter maintenance specialist and an infant-care facilitator. We learn he shovels snow and babysits. Lastly, his resume states that he has worked with others in a supervisory capacity. We learn he hired his sister once to sweep the garage. The good news is, the employer is so impressed with his ability to embellish the truth that he gets the job. Other times, it's difficult for both the Exaggerator and the listener to distinguish fact from fiction. As trust, respect and integrity may be involved here, relationship building may be difficult. It's easy for the Exaggerator to either turn you on or off with his embellishments. If they turn you on, then they have to live up to the image they've created.

How to deal with the Experts

- learn from their strengths
- take what they know and do well, and use it well
- ignore their arrogance if it serves your purpose
- enjoy the ride (even the bumps)
- don't take it personally

If you're an Expert:

- look at your behaviour: do people feel comfortable with you or are you pushing them away? turning them on? turning them off?
- if you need to make a change, run through the change process in Chapter 1, and make a decision to do so

Follow-up Questions

➤ What's one effective technique for dealing with a Perfectionist who is perpetually on your case?

➤ Do you point out to Know-It-Alls that they don't know everything, or do you let them think they do?

➤ How much time and energy do you put into trying to persuade an Inflexible?

---

3. The Reactors

The Reactors are emotionally triggered by certain words, phrases, people and situations. Examples of emotional reactions are: anger, joy, sadness, jealousy, and fear.

The Reactors fall into four groups:

i) The Needies

ii) The Blamers

iii) The Grudge Holders

iv) The Grenades

i) The Needies

The Needies need your recognition, your appreciation, your consideration, your validation and your stamp of approval. Be on the alert for the person who comes to a meeting with a fishing rod and no bait, but wants to catch a lot of fish.

EXAMPLE

Carl grew up in a home where his father was an absolute perfectionist. And nothing Carl ever did was "good enough." As a result, Carl became sensitive to criticism of any kind, especially when it was given in an angry, sarcastic way which resembled his father's speaking style.

ANALYSIS

Although an adult, Carl still feels like a victim, like he did as a child when he was unable to protect or defend himself against his father. As an adult, he is still hooked on this feeling, and has been unable to stop reacting. He's especially sensitive to people who give feedback in an angry, sarcastic way as his father did. Moreover, Carl is constantly looking to others for validation and approval.

What Are Your Triggers?

1. List words and phrases that you have an emotional reaction to (both positive and negative reactions; be honest):

   Examples:
   – you're lazy
   – you can't you ever do anything right
   – just leave me alone
   – you're emotional
   – I don't have time for you/this
   – what makes you think you're so important?
   – you're stupid
   – you think you're better than everyone else
   – fatso
   – wimp
   – cheapskate
   – you should ...
   – proud
   – browner

– teacher's pet
– you're a dumb jock
– you're so messy
– you only care about yourself
– you're ugly
– so, we're not good enough for you
– act like a man
– act like a lady
– don't be such a baby
– stop being silly
– you come on too strong

2. List the kind of people that you have an emotional reaction to (both positive and negative reactions; be honest):

   Examples:
   – remind you of your grandmother
   – remind you of your grandfather
   – remind you of your mother
   – remind you of your father
   – remind you of your brother
   – remind you of your sister
   – people who always smile
   – people who never smile
   – people who are sarcastic
   – people who are petty
   – people who are unkind
   – people who are self-absorbed
   – people in suits
   – people in jeans
   – people who are overweight
   – people who are underweight
   – people who are closed-minded
   – people who are narrow-minded
   – people who don't appreciate the little things
   – people who are black and white
   – people who are disrespectful
   – people who want something for nothing
   – people who are always in a hurry
   – people who won't get involved
   – others (list):

3. List the kinds of situations that prompt an emotional reaction in you (example: school type settings, family outings and gatherings, sad books, funny movies, blues music, religious settings; be honest).

4. List any family, friends and business people who conjure up an immediate reaction in you when you hear their name(s), their voice(s). Be honest.

ii) The Grudge Holders

"Life is too short to hold grudges. To be able to forgive can be enormously healing and life-enhancing. It's the best example of casting your bread upon the waters and getting back caviar sandwiches."

- Ann Landers

Grudge Holders allow their resentment of a person or an issue to fester and grow. Often a pin-prick problem becomes a bomb as the grudge builds over time.

EXAMPLE

A group of friends decide to throw a last-minute surprise birthday bash for their friend Alan. They give all the invitees the same three-day notice and extend their apologies for the short notice and their disorganization. Dan, one of the invitees, can't change his plans and can't come to the bash. He is angry and will hold a grudge against the organizers for not giving him more lead time.

ANALYSIS

Dan has taken a situation that arose out of disorganization and reacted to it personally. He is holding a grudge which is beneficial to no one. Least of all himself!

Remember! Holding a grudge is a useless emotion that keeps you stuck in the past.

iii) The Blamers

"Take charge of your thoughts, you can do what you will with them."

- Plato

Blamers dodge all accountability. Their school of thought is, "It couldn't be me. It must be the other guy." In Jeff MacNelly's comic strip *Shoe,* we see a gent at his desk buried in mounds of paper. He asks the operator to help him locate a listing for "Messy Desks Anonymous." When nothing turns up, he tries a self-help organization, a hotline for people who are organizationally challenged, and a support group. Again, when nothing turns up, he admits to the operator that he's looking for someone else to blame the big mess on.

EXAMPLE 1

Daughter: Why don't you *ever* listen to me?

Father: What are you starting? *You're just like your mother.*

Daughter: Well, you didn't listen to me when I was very young before I got to know what my mother was like.

Father (no response).

ANALYSIS

Humour aside, this father creates an opportunity to lay blame not on one person but two — mother and daughter — and refuses to look at his behaviour.

And another all-too-true blamer story just for fun:

EXAMPLE 2

Colette walks down several flights of steps to the basement level of her apartment building to retrieve her mail. She opens the basement door and bumps into a tenant on route to get her mail.

Colette (sincerely): I'm *terribly* sorry. Are you hurt?

Ann (angry, rubbing her arm): *No.*

Colette (sincerely and concerned that Ann's been hurt): You were walking very close to the door.

Ann (angry): Well, I didn't know you were going to open it.

Colette (pleasantly assertive): That's what doors are for: they open and they close.

ANALYSIS

Colette showed "beyond the call" concern for this careless pedestrian. Angry with herself for walking so close to the door and for getting hurt, Ann laid blame on Colette and tried to make her feel worse than she already did.

Remember! The word blame contains the word "lame." The word "lame" contains the word "me."

iv) The Grenades

Grenades generally explode in a burst of anger when they are triggered. Their behaviour may also appear self-righteous and hurtful to others.

EXAMPLE 1

Amy is telling Louise about a family situation after the fact. Amy is not asking for advice or anything else. Louise's role as a friend is simply to listen. Watch what happens when a grenade explodes.

Amy (pleasant, making conversation): I got in touch with my sister in Germany yesterday. I've been concerned about my parents. Her being there and me here, and I needed to ask her a few questions about how we will take care of our parents in an emergency. It would be *much easier* if she were home.

Louise (indignant, self-righteous, interrupting Amy): *You don't have the right to tell your sister to come home*. You're here, and that means you're responsible for them.

Amy (calmly): The questions I asked my sister were not related to her decision to come home or when to come home. We discussed how we'd jointly handle an emergency in her absence in the best interests of our parents, taking both our personal and professional situations into consideration. (Amy then quickly ends the conversation.)

Louise pulls back and reflects. They are quiet for several minutes, and then another conversation starts.

ANALYSIS

Louise, the grenade is reacting instantaneously to a situation she's been in many times over. Her Self-Protector listening mask on, Louise asks no questions; rather, she makes assumptions and cuts in. Louise who sees herself as a victim, feels everyone should simply accept the situation they're in and "make the best of it." She comes from the "grin and bear it because you have no options" school of thought.

Amy, on the other hand, believes that she and her sister have joint custody of their aging parents, and so she looked to her sister for role clarification if and when something should go wrong during her sister's absence. Amy's response was systematic, practical and caring about everyone involved. Amy responded to Louise strategically and calmly. Had she reacted with heightened emotion, this situation could have easily escalated and Amy, who was simply sharing something important with a friend, could have been hurt. Louise was not asked for advice nor was it her place to offer any. Her job at that moment in time was just to listen to her friend. Amy has now learned one of Louise's grenade-like triggers and will stay clear in sharing anything of this nature with her again.

EXAMPLE 2

Sandra and Malcolm had a miscommunication on a project they had worked on together. They got the job done, but they had never cleared the air. Sandra called a short meeting to do so a couple of days after the project was complete. Here is their follow-up conversation.

Sandra (sincerely): I wanted to clear the air on the Smithmore project. I misinterpreted what you had said about our project expenses. I don't filter information well when people scream; I grew up with a full-time screamer. When you lost your temper and screamed at me, I took it personally.

Malcolm (giving Sandra credit): I apologize.

(Sandra smiles at Malcolm and he returns the smile.)

ANALYSIS

Malcolm was caught up in his own frustration and emotional needs and couldn't meet Sandra's. She reacted to Malcolm's screaming, immediately put on her Self-Protector listening mask and, therefore, couldn't properly filter the contents of the message itself. She took it personally. When she had a chance to reassess the situation, she tackled the problem head on.

Remember! Water drowns fire, and a calm and quiet tone and style can transform a firebreather into a pussycat.

How to deal with the Reactors

- respond (facts and feelings) don't react (feelings): make sure you always model your behaviour opposite to theirs
- stay focused on the goal of the discussion
- don't reinforce their behaviour
- don't bait the hook
- stay cool and calm
- enjoy the ride (even the bumps)
- don't take it personally

If you're a Reactor:

➤ Recognize that you're reacting.* Ask yourself some helpful questions and get in touch with your feelings:

---

* Note: If you can catch the trigger in time (sort of like nipping a migraine while enroute), do so. If the trigger does go off, immediately correct the damage, take responsibility for your words and deeds, and stay in the present tense.

- Why am I (bothered, elated, scared, angry, etc.)?
- Why am I so intense?
- My stomach is in knots; why?
- I'm not usually like this; what's going on?
- Am I taking this personally? What's it got to do with me?
- Why am I so offended?
- Why did I come on so strong?
- Why am I upset; this isn't my issue, but it struck a chord.
- Why does it feel so close to home?
- I feel sad.
- I feel scared.
- I feel worried.
- I feel angry.
- I feel self-pity.
- I feel regret.

➤ Ask yourself if your behaviour is moving the situation forward:
   - Have we accomplished anything in the discussion?
   - Have we accomplished anything in the friendship?
   - Where do we productively go from here?

➤ Make a decision to change your behaviour if it's not moving the situation forward.

Follow-up Questions

➤ List one situation where you helped the Reactor to change his or her behaviour.
➤ List any people you know who are always coming to you for pats on the back.
➤ What methods have you found effective in dealing with Blamers?

4. The Complainers

The Complainers allow their feelings to control the facts. They like to get carried away, mope and whine, and have others indulge them. Some complainers have an "I deserve" mentality and think that everything is coming to them.

The Complainers fall into four groups:

i)   The Whiners

ii) The Martyrs

iii) Los Negativos

iv) The Takers

i) The Whiners

As we first saw in Chapter 4, Whiners mull over the same issue 1,000 times, complain, *kvetch*, complain again, *kvetch* again, yet never do anything to fix the problem(s). They don't want to or don't feel they can — or both. They are prone to self-pity and are notorious for talk-at-you monologues, but don't mean to burden or offend.

EXAMPLE

Following is a Sunday morning telephone dialogue between Isla and her mother Mrs. Beck which illustrates the whiner syndrome.

Mrs. Beck: Hello.

Isla: Hi mother, how are things going?

Mrs. Beck: Same old thing. Get up in the morning, go to bed at night. I guess it could be worse. I shouldn't complain.

Isla: Well, I wanted to know if you'd like to go for a coffee this morning.

Mrs. Beck: Well, I'm not feeling so hotsy totsy. My back's bothering me, but that's nothing new. My sugar level is up again, I can't lose any weight and I have nothing to do. And now they tell me I have to start with a nutritionist. What can I tell you?

ANALYSIS

Basically, a good soul and unwittingly funny, Mrs. Beck is a chronic whiner who never changes, doesn't listen, doesn't really want any solutions — but always expects you to listen to her kvetch.

ii) The Martyrs

Martyrs are always sacrificing themselves for the good of others. Selfless in their actions, they can also cause themselves a lot of unnecessary grief for the "good of the cause." This also gives them something to complain about, and is their way of gaining approval and acceptance.

EXAMPLE

At 5:00 p.m. on a Friday, Sally Carter took a stand. She was head of the geography department at a 3,000-plus high school. To bail out a team of 10 teachers, none of whom was willing to teach an extra tutorial session that had to run first semester, Sally undertook the course. She was never compensated in time, money or appreciation by management or her colleagues.

When Sally's second semester schedule came out, management had deleted Sally's previously negotiated field trip money. Sally was up in arms and went to the principal to discuss the situation. The conversation went like this:

Sally: I taught an extra tutorial for you first semester, *I bailed the staff out,* was not paid for it and now you're trying to take my field trip money away.

Peter: I don't remember you offering to take on the extra tutorial, and neither does anyone else.

Sally: I feel *very used* Peter, and I want to know what you are going to do about it.

Peter: Well, I don't want you to feel that way but I'm sure I didn't ask you to do something without offering to pay for it. I would never do anything like that. But I appreciate that you see it that way. But why don't you have a letter from Jerry (the school's federation president) that says you agreed to take on the extra course?

Sally: I asked Jerry to write the letter three times and he never did. I'm not stupid, Peter. When I was department head last year, I negotiated an increase for Marilyn who taught an extra course.

Peter: Well, I've got a whole set of new field equipment.

Sally: You can't *buy me off* with a set of equipment, Peter.

ANALYSIS

As you can appreciate, there were many dimensions to this conversation and it is still not resolved. But the bottom line is that Peter refused to give Sally credit either in time or compensation for her extra work and also refused to give her back the prep class that had been deleted.

To retain her integrity, Sally decided not to try and get Peter to pay her back. She did her work and nothing extra for awhile until the hurt and disappointment subsided. She would only be hurting herself if she continued to feel this way. And she didn't want her students to suffer for the staff's lack of support and the principal's lack of principles.

Sally mistakenly trusted that the people she worked with operated with the same level of integrity as she did. She also mistakenly assumed they appreciated her special effort to bail them out. When they were all asked for their support on the issue, no one could remember what had happened as it was several months ago.

Sally was left burnt out and ill, and she lost a lot of respect for the principal, the school's federation president and the staff.

WRAP-UP

In talking through the situation with Sally, she concluded that next time she'd look after herself in writing and make sure she gets paid for her work, and learn from this mistake.

Remember! No one can take advantage of you unless you let them. If you act like a doormat, people will wipe their feet on you.

iii) Los Negativos

As a rule, man is a fool.
When it's hot, he wants it cool.
When it's cool, he wants it hot.
Always wanting what is not.
- Anon.

Los Negativos always tune into the downside of everything. For them, the cup is always half empty rather than half full. They are never happy or satisfied or pleased with what is and always want something more, something less, something other, something else. They *kvetch* for the sake of it, and intend to create a negative spiral effect:

–   when the sun is shining, it's too hot
–   when the sun is not shining, it's too cold
–   when they want to buy something, you offer them a good price and they say they don't want it and do you have another colour

– when they just land a great, challenging job with a good salary and benefits they focus on the fact that "it's too much work," "takes too many hours," or is "too hard."

EXAMPLE 1

Following is part of a conversation Marjorie had with one of her "old" friends last Christmas.

Marjorie: Hi, Juliana. I called to wish you and yours all the best over the holidays.

Juliana: Oh hi, Marjorie. I haven't heard from you *in a long time.* (Tone: and I hope you feel extremely guilty about it. Four months had passed and neither party had called.)

Marjorie (no guilt and sincere): I didn't get around to sending personal Christmas cards this year and you're on my phone list. So, how is everything?

Juliana: Fine ... Well, things are *slow* at work, my husband is trying to build his business, we're *slowly* paying off our $1,000-a -month mortgage. I can't afford daycare for my two-and-a-half-year old because my husband and I earn over $60K. And $60K is the government cutoff for funding. And I don't think the cutoff is fair considering we have five in our family ... and ...

ANALYSIS

I think you understand why Marjorie picks up the phone only a couple of times a year. Although there are many sunny spots (including an inexpensive $1,000-a-month mortgage and a $75K household income), all Juliana sees is a constant negative and "slow" downpour. To boot, her family of five includes her mother whom she sponsored from another country to live with them and look after her two children! Los Negativos are always unhappy, no matter what. Even when things are good, and everyone is happy and healthy.

EXAMPLE 2

Harriet, an inspections manager in a pharmaceutical company, has been unhappy in her job for several years. She hit the glass ceiling, several years ago, took a blow to her confidence — yet stayed. In the last few months, she decided to make a move and found a terrific new position with a competitor. During her last week she "dumped her bag" on the Human Resources manager on all the "injustices" that were happening in her department — and specifically the injustices that had happened to her. She complained about the "lack of compliments" she was given in the leaving notice that was posted, the department's lack of interest in making her a formal good-bye, and the quality of the gift she received upon departure. Nothing was acceptable.

ANALYSIS

In reality, she should have been jumping up and down at her pending departure. In addition, she had a lovely long-distance chat with the division vice-president, who specifically called just to send her off. Folks in her department gave her a lovely send-off, including lunch and a gift, and she had personal good-byes with everyone in the company whom she cared about. Three important questions come to mind:

➤ Why did Harriet stay for so long when the fit was not good for her?

➤ Why did she wait until she was leaving to spill the beans?

➤ If she understood the unhappy campers in her department so well (the reason she was leaving), why was she disappointed with her send-off?

Harriet's Process

Harriet worked with a coach, Margaret, in making her decision to look for a new job. Following is a section of the report written by Margaret:

> "I remember helping Harriet who was totally frustrated with her career. She felt stuck, had reached the glass ceiling and her confidence was eroding. Over a period of several months, I encouraged her to take care of her needs, and to make a long-overdue move — to find a place for herself where she could grow her skills.
>
> "At first, I was bombarded with a 101 excuses all leading to the point that she had a certain level of comfort in her uncomfortable situation and wasn't sure she wanted to let it go. She'd almost come to be happy being unhappy. She'd become used to habitual suffering and didn't know how to give it up. Finally, she decided to give up the pain and to be fair to herself. My first conversation with her once she was installed in her new job went something like this:
>
> Margaret: Hi there. I just called to see how the new job's going.

Harriet: Oh, Margaret. I have *so much work* I can't believe it. Had I known they were going to throw me in so fast, I wouldn't have taken it. I'm just ...

Margaret: Are you enjoying it?

Harriet: Oh yes (audible sigh), but it's just *so much work*. I have no time for anything. Had I known ...

WRAP-UP

I think you get the drift. Margaret cut her off quickly (in true Lion fashion) because she saw no point in reinforcing her negative behaviour. She was looking for major sympathy for all her "hard work." Her coach ended the conversation with, "I hope you continue to find it challenging." A month went by and there was no word from Harriet, so Margaret called. And she was still complaining. About what? About creating a super opportunity for herself, leading to upper management, with a generous salary and benefit package? Her coach stopped calling. SWSWSWN — some will, some won't, so what. Next. And in this case, as Billy Crystal said in the movie *The Princess Bride*, "It'll take a miracle!"[21]

iv) The Takers

"It seems like everyone has an "I deserve" mentality these days. What does anyone deserve? All the people I know who are happy and successful have worked hard for it. And work hard to maintain it."

- A civil servant,
in conversation with the author

Takers have an "I deserve" mentality and feel that things are coming to them. *Chutzpah* is a wonderful word in Yiddish that describes someone who is assertive and goes after what he wants. But the Takers go way beyond *Chutzpah* — they have been blessed with unmitigated gall and nerve and cheek galore, and simply don't know when to let up.

Do any of these sound familiar? Have any of them happened to you in some shape or form? Here are a few example of "beyond Chutzpah," the ultimate taker in action.

➤ A couple and their two children are returning to the wife's country of origin for a holiday. The flight is free with their frequent-flyer points and they have free room and board and full use of a vehicle on the other side. The husband complains about the cost involved in buying presents for his wife's family and friends!

➤ A customer buys four plates on sale. She carefully examines them, buys them and asks for gift wrap. The store manager tells the customer that they don't gift wrap but that she'd be happy to wrap the plates for her if she purchases the wrappings at the dollar store across the street. The customer does so. The store manager is busy wrapping away and the customer says, "Will you fold the corners differently. I don't like the way you are wrapping it!"

➤ You've been standing in line for tickets for a half an hour. You're about number 25 in line. Out of nowhere, a man rushes to the front of the line claiming to see an old friend who's second in line!

➤ A family is moving from South Africa to Canada. They have a container of items that is being shipped. Friends ask if they can include "a little something" for a daughter in Toronto. The folks who are moving respond "with pleasure." However, it was not a pleasure when they arrived with a five-piece bedroom suite and a 9-foot x 12-foot carpet!

EXAMPLE

During one of Herbert's visits to an advertising company, he noticed a lovely print hanging in the lobby. He mentioned how much he liked it to the receptionist. Her response was as follows.

Receptionist: Yes, I really like it, too. Actually, it would look *great* in my apartment. I was thinking of asking for it.

Herbert: Really? That's interesting. Why?

Receptionist: Well, I look at it every day, and I think they should give it to me.

Herbert (a knowing smile): Oh.

ANALYSIS

Stuck in the entitlement trap, this receptionist believes her employer owes her something — other than a salary commensurate with her job. A chronic complaint of employers is that there are an overwhelming number of employees who believe that by doing just enough to get by, and by being around long enough, entitles them to a raise or promotion — or even free artwork.

Remember! The taker can only take if you give. It's up to you to draw the line and set limits for the taker.

How to deal with the Complainers

- put on your selective listening mask
- listen briefly
- don't reinforce their behaviour
- don't get taken in
- laugh a lot
- enjoy the ride (even the bumps)
- don't take it personally

If you're a Complainer:

- notice others' reactions and responses to your comments and behaviour
- ask yourself if this is what you want
- ask yourself if there is something you want and need to change, and review the change process

Follow-up Questions

➤ How do you learn to set limits with Complainers?
➤ What prompts people to become Martyrs?
➤ Is there hope for Los Negativos?

---

5. The Pleasers

Pleasers work hard to be liked and accepted. They're quick to lend a helping hand, will back down from a confrontation to keep the peace, and generally do and say nice things. They want you to feel comfortable and accepted and go out of their way to create this atmosphere. During the break at a workshop, a pleaser may go out and get a coffee for everyone, or fill up everyone's water glass.

The Pleasers fall into four groups:

i) The Yes Persons
ii) The Conformists
iii) The Do-It-Alls
iv) The Fabricators

Some typical Pleasers are:

➤ the person who asks his roommate to get rid of his cat because the superintendent is making a fuss (even though the by-law states that you can have a cat in your apartment)

➤ the person who has her friends over for Christmas morning brunch when she really wants to do Christmas dinner (but then, so did her friend)

➤ the person who allows out-of-town relatives to drop in "any time"

➤ the person who runs a 24-hour airport pickup and delivery service for family and friends

➤ the person who immediately responds with a gift when he receives one

➤ the person who always gives compliments

➤ the person who always agrees with you because you're the boss

➤ the person who complains about a procedure, but when you confront him, he won't state his opinion

➤ the person who won't say anything during a conflict situation to avoid hurt feelings

➤ the person who agrees to most things as they are small issues and not worth fussing over (e.g., where to sit at the movies, where to go to eat).

i) The Yes Person

"My idea of an agreeable person is one who agrees with me."

- Samuel Johnson

The Yes Person is totally gutless and won't take a stand on anything. Doesn't have an opinion or at least pretends not to have one. Just says "yes" to whatever is asked of him or her. Yes People avoid conflict at all costs. In Bill Holbrook's *On the Fastrack* comic strip, Rose Trellis and her protégé Bob Shirt are guests on a talk show. The show host asks what makes their company Fastrack special, and Rose defers to Bob to take the question who answers "Yes, Ms. Trellis." Bob goes on to explain that at Fastrack they've created an atmosphere where everyone is treated with the same standard of human respect and dignity, that they encourage independent thinking and don't teach blind obedience. Rose says, "Very good, Bob." He thanks her, and she offers him a cookie.

ii) The Do-It-Alls

The ardent parent, friend, teacher, homemaker, doctor and social worker for example who "does it all" and tries to please their spouse, kids, parents, friends, colleagues, high school acquaintances, three charities and society at large. Setting limits can be hard to do if you're a Do-It-All.

EXAMPLE

Martin stayed on the phone with a business acquaintance for one hour trying to help him go through a process for finding work as he'd been caught in three downsizings and was desperate. Eager to help and to please, like most Pleasers, Martin had difficulty dealing with three minutes of effusive thank yous. As his friend's self-esteem had been hit, and he wanted to repay Martin's kindness, he overdid it on the thank yous and Martin became uncomfortable. As well, Martin was angry with himself for giving too much time and not knowing when to stop. By the time he got off the telephone, he was beat and had neglected some of his own priorities.

EXAMPLE

Thelma: Here's the copy of the report you asked me for.

Drake: Thank you very much, but I didn't *expect it* so soon. I haven't gotten around to duplicating that proposal for you. *Priorities*, you know. But I'll try my very best this week.

Thelma: Oh, that's okay.

ANALYSIS

Secretly folks, Thelma is fuming. She felt that if she rushed to get Drake his stuff he should have put himself out to get back to her. In reality, no deadlines were set here, but Thelma took it personally that she wasn't higher on his priority list, and inadvertently set herself up for a fall.

iii) The Conformists

Conformists don't like to make waves and they want to be part of the crowd and to be liked and accepted. We see people conform to aspects of corporate culture (e.g., everyone is in the cafeteria for a coffee and muffin by 8:00 a.m.), dress to conform (uniform, conservative, casual), conforming behaviour (intense, low key, enthusiastic, passive), conforming ideas (agree with the powers that be).

EXAMPLE 1

Theresa has a big family and there are frequent get-togethers for birthdays and holidays. Constantly bombarded with gifts, Theresa asked that her guests "bring themselves only and no gifts for her four-year-old" when they attend a family get-together. As a result, her friends and relatives went from buying big-ticket items to smaller gifts. Big dolls became smaller dolls and so on. Last Christmas, Theresa packed up piles of stuff and dropped them off at a children's shelter. This was great for the children at the shelter, but why didn't her family and friends believe her when she said "no gifts"?

ANALYSIS

These Conformists are adhering to what they feel are appropriate cultural and societal norms related to gift-giving. They would "not feel right" attending a gathering where a child was present without bringing a present.

EXAMPLE 2

After major surgery, Andrea is in a coma and is being kept alive and medicated intravenously. Andrea's best friend Pat has Power of Attorney and she wants to give Andrea every chance to survive. Andrea's semi-estranged brother John is notified and arrives from overseas and demands that his sister be allowed to die. John stays at Andrea's apartment during his 10-day visit, takes several mementos from the apartment without permission, demands that his airfare be paid (Pat complies) and returns home, stating he will not be returning upon Andrea's death. Andrea is moved to a palliative care unit and dies within two weeks.

ANALYSIS

To keep the peace, Pat complies with all of John's wishes, but feels angry, resentful, helpless and hopeless during and after John's visit.

iv) The Fabricators

Fabricators will embellish the truth (just a touch) to make the other person feel good. They say things like:

- Turquoise is definitely your colour (the jacket was awful so the pleaser focused on the colour).
- It looks like you've lost a few inches (you've gained three).
- Good tie. Nice colours (when the tie's three inches too wide).
- You're looking well! (like death warmed over).

How to deal with the Pleaser

- don't try to keep up with them (you'll get pooped)
- never take advantage of them
- never take them for granted
- enjoy the ride (even the bumps)
- never take it personally

If you're a Pleaser:

- give what you want to give when you want to give it
- make sure you feel the balance in the friendship
- don't expect others to please you as you do them (that's an unrealistic expectation)
- don't forget to take care of yourself and to please yourself once in a while

Follow-up Questions

➤ How do you deal with a Pleaser who is constantly "giving" and "doing" in the relationship?

➤ How can you encourage a Pleaser to take a little more?

➤ What is a Pleaser's worst fear?

6. The Pricklies

Pricklies are prickly on the outside, mushy on the inside. Their heads and hearts are in the right places. They come through on all the important things, but others don't see always this because they can have a gruff exterior.

The Pricklies fall into four groups:

i) The No-Trespassers
ii) The Vulnerables
iii) The Gruffer the Toughers
iv) The Worriers

Some typical Pricklies are:

➤ The awesome police officer who gives you a break for a first-time moving violation without your asking.

➤ The hard-nosed service advisor at the garage who grunts a good morning but is sure to have your car out by noon because he knows you need it for work.

➤ The diligent teacher who walks a hard line to make sure the students get what they need and gives no breaks, yet is always there when a student needs a helping hand.

➤ The nurse who is outwardly rude and abrupt, but is there immediately when needed.

➤ The military officer who's miserable to deal with, but would sacrifice his life for any member of his platoon.

➤ The manager who doesn't ask his staff how they are every day, but will fight to the death if one of them has an issue he strongly believes in.

➤ The supervisor who cuts you off in mid-sentence many a day, but hears your child is sick and tells you to leave early.

➤ The tough-as-nails property manager of a condominium complex who gives a homeowner a plant from the lobby because she liked it.

i) The No-Trespassers

These Pricklies shut you out when it comes to their real feelings. The No-Trespasser, for example, will become a Big Brother and help to change his little brother's life, but even when asked, won't tell the little brother why it was so important for him to be his Big Brother. Generous to a fault, it is hard for them to share their real feelings.

ii) The Vulnerables

The Vulnerables have very good hearts and are always putting themselves in a position where they could be taken advantage of. Helpful and caring, they are vulnerable to people in pain, emotional or otherwise, people who are ill, people who are fearful, need protection, and people who just don't stand on their own two feet. They have trained themselves to use the Self-Protector listening mask to protect themselves — but often don't do such a good job — and can fall prey to looking after everyone — and can neglect themselves in the process.

iii) The Gruffer the Toughers

For the Gruffer the Toughers, being kind is easy. For example, although he often has a ferocious bark on a daily basis (chides teenagers waiting in the apartment lobby), an apartment building superintendent prearranges with four tenants to carry an ill tenant from the eighth floor of the apartment building in case of emergency. He's always there when you *really* need him.

iv) The Worriers

The Worriers take too much responsibility for the outcome of a situation. They try so hard to be the ardent caretakers, are always rushing over with chicken soup when you're sick, worrying about your happiness, worrying about your success, worrying about your love life. You name it. They worry. They care.

How to deal with the Pricklies

- understand that they care and want to help
- show you appreciate them
- never take advantage of them
- enjoy the ride (even the bumps)
- never take it personally

If you're a Prickly:

- show your vulnerabilities at the right time, with the right people
- let people stand on their own two feet
- take care of yourself: self-preservation is the key (you're no good to anyone if you don't take care of yourself first)

Follow-up Questions

- ➤ Do Pricklies focus on words or actions?
- ➤ List three good ways to establish rapport with a Prickly.
- ➤ Do you have any pricklies as friends? Are you a Prickly?

10 Affirmations to Prepare Yourself for Dealing with Challenging Personalities

1. I am responsible for my results; others for their results.
2. Others can only hurt or disappoint me if I let them.
3. I am in control of how I think and feel.
4. I am self-committed and know what I want and need.
5. I am responsible for my feelings of self-worth.
6. I can conquer any dragons in my head.
7. I'm consciously competent: I know what I'm good at and what areas I can grow in.
8. I do not need anyone's approval but my own.
9. I take the time to respond not react.
10. I am responsible for my feelings; others are responsible for theirs.

Remember! The world is full of daily challenges and challenging people with challenging personalities. By understanding the way these personalities interact, you can create successful interactions and relationships.

So Strategy 8 of the *How Not To Take It Personally Action Plan* is to get to know the Six Types of Challenging Personalities and all their sub-types.

Let's review the four steps to increase our knowledge and apply them.

1. Identify the Challenging Personalities.
2. Design strategies for dealing with them.
3. Decide if you are one of the challenging personalities, and if others see you this way.
4. Look at your behaviour in light of your results in dealing with people and see if there's anything you might like to change.

CHAPTER 9

TECHNOLOGY CAN ENHANCE COMMUNICATION

"We are in an era of tremendous change. The merging of voice and data technologies is transforming communications, in effect making the world smaller and more intimate, and providing all of us — at business and at home — with a more pervasive, powerful and flexible means of exchanging information."

- Bob Cohn, *Chairman & CEO,*
Octel Communications

Strategy 9: Choose the Right Medium for your Message

This chapter will deal with the use of spoken and written language with the appropriate technological medium. Our goal is to keep our communication human (combine the facts and the feelings well) and simultaneously to increase productivity on the job. How can we eliminate some of the 70 percent of workplace errors that stem from a lack of quality communication?

I remember a not-so-funny incident where two vice-presidents were battling on the E-mail, and both were copying the president. In frustration, the president called them both into the office to get to the bottom of the E-mail war. As a result my client, the vice-president of finance, went to the vice-president of marketing to finally "communicate and fix the problem." The vice-president of marketing attributed the problem to their both being stubborn (which appeared to be the case); they quickly solved the problem and left it at that.

Over lunch with the vice-president of finance, I asked him why he pursued the E-mail war. He said he knew he was doing the wrong thing, but he was angry and just got caught up in firing off the messages. He is not alone. Even at his level. Miscommmunications such as this one happen regularly. They impact on productivity.

We will discuss the use of spoken and written language with the following three technologies:

1. Voice Mail (IVMS) — Integrated Voice Messaging Systems*
2. Electronic Mail (E-mail)
3. Fax (written memos, proposals, reports)

TO SPEAK OR TO WRITE — THAT IS THE QUESTION

As we discussed in Chapter 4, spoken English is dynamic and conveys meaning in the moment. In this sense, we can think of speaking as a metaphor for activity. Written language, on the other hand, simply "is" or "exists," and is a metaphor for the tangible things we've created in the world.[22] Where written language is the car, spoken language is the activity of driving. Both represent different dimensions of language and how we experience life. And both modes of language are necessary in business and our busy, complex world.

Linguist Michael Halliday (1985) says that what is communicated by speaking and what is communicated by writing aren't identical. We learn through language, and some kinds of learning take place more effectively through spoken language and some through written. Although both writing and speaking operate with the same linguistic underpinnings, they use different features of language (features of spoken English were discussed in Chapter 4), and so differently influence their audience. As a result, the spoken and written modes of language give us options on how to best get through to people. There's a time to voice mail and a time to fax. There's a time to E-mail and there's a time for a face-to-face.

COMMUNICATING BY, THROUGH AND WITH TECHNOLOGY

When using technology to enhance our communication we need to take three things into consideration:

---

* Note: Voice mail naturally uses spoken English and E-mail and faxing use colloquial written English (sounds like everyday spoken English), as well as standard forms of written English based on the audience, purpose, content and situation.

➤ different people have different learning styles

➤ different people are more comfortable with certain mediums based on their aptitude and attitude

➤ different mediums are more appropriate for some kinds of messages (don't try to do a spreadsheet on voice mail!).

The Three Learning Styles

Some people are high aural/oral learners (they receive information quickly through their ears and then learn from listening to their own output and the output of others). Visual learners learn by watching, reading and by focusing on word pictures. Tactile learners learn by jumping in, getting their hands dirty and doing. They like to see what they are getting. As you can appreciate, we are all bits and pieces of each learning style. Equally, we all have at least one predominant learning style and generally a secondary learning style.

What's your best guess?

1. Will the tactile learner prefer shorter or longer messages?

   Would they prefer their messages face-to-face, on voice mail or E-mail? How would the tactile learner respond to a short fax? Long fax?

2. Will the visual learner be more receptive to voice mail or to E-mail?

3. For the aural/oral learner, in what medium will you have the most impact?

Our Aptitude

Aptitude predisposes people to learn certain skills better and more quickly than others. Aptitude could include things like general learning ability, vocabulary, problem solving and number manipulation, the ability to see three dimensions in a two-dimensional representation, the ability to register form (you see a hammer and then recall the outline), motor co-ordination, finger dexterity and manual dexterity.

A person's aptitude or inherent traits (the ones you're born with) in technology define his or her technological potential. People who have an interest and aptitude for technology will have a quicker learning curve. Equally, those with a lower technological aptitude will tend to pick up on things more slowly and may even avoid using technology altogether. As humans, we are motivated to do what we are good at because it reinforces our belief in ourselves.

And based on our aptitude, some people are more or less effective in a particular medium. Are you more predisposed to the telephone, face-to-face, or written communication? Minus visual input, some people are unable to get an accurate reading on the person and the situation. Others are far more effective on the telephone than in writing, and so gravitate to voice mail over E-mail where possible. Others still prefer the telephone to face-to-face or written interaction.

Our Judgement and Common Sense

Our judgement and common sense (part of our aptitude) complement our technical training, and the protocol systems used at and with different organizations. Sound judgement and common sense help us to choose the appropriate medium, message and tone. Technology doesn't replace critical thinking, but it certainly can help us to enhance it.

Both judgement and common sense are inherent skills (you're born with them), and I'm sure you've met people who have a surplus of either or both, and conversely those who appear to be short-changed. The good news is, regardless of how much you've got to start, these inherent traits can be honed through self-awareness and communication skill building, and through a thorough orientation with the technology itself.

An example where someone has not necessarily exercised the best judgement would be a human resources assistant who consistently sends the human resource manager up to 20 voice-mail messages daily when their offices are side by side! A frequent complaint.

Same Message, Multiple Mediums

Judgement also comes into play when selecting multiple mediums for the same message and/or multiple audiences for the same message. Some people will send a voice-mail message, an E-mail message and a hard copy all on the same issue and to multiple audiences, and flood their organization. Using solid judgement with technology helps companies save time, money and legal bills.

1. Multiple messages waste resources and overload voice-mail and E-mail systems. Productivity is affected.

2. Multiple messages can engender a "lack of trust" and destroy the solidarity of language and likemindedness that we talked about in Chapter 4, to the point of hurting or permanently hindering a relationship. Frequent comments I've heard in organizations include things like:

"Doesn't she trust me to get this done? Why is she reminding me on voice mail? I just got her E-mail yesterday, printed it off and have it in front of me. *I can read.*"

"I don't know why he had to send me a follow-up fax on this. We discussed it and I know what I have to do. *Does he think I'm stupid?*"

"She doesn't know when to back off. I got the abridged story on voice mail, and now she's giving me every detail of the same issue on my E-mail. *Where is she coming from?*"

"He always tells me the same thing at least twice. Does he think *I'm irresponsible* and don't know how to meet a deadline?"

As you know, it's easy to interpret these double messages as personal slights. And yes, sometimes they may be intended to be just that. But for the vast majority of our messages, if we don't take them personally, people's mindsets will become clear. We will discover that in doubling up on a message, most people want to:

➤ show their commitment to the issue or project

➤ engender commitment in the receiver

➤ create a sense of urgency about the issue or project and instill this in the receiver

➤ convey an important content and relationship message to the receiver: you're good, this issue or project is important to me and I want it to be important for you too, and I'm glad we're working on it together.

Showing You Care in Writing

Once, at a business writing workshop I ran at Ryerson Polytechnic University, this whole notion of commitment and urgency came up. One very frustrated participant was discussing how some people reacted to her written messages. She was constantly plagued with feedback like "you're too aggressive," "you're too pushy," "you're too demanding." When I asked her if she felt this was true, she very thoughtfully and poignantly answered, "I care." And the room was filled with audible, "I know just how you feel" sighs.

Her comment opened up a whole discussion for us on how to show you care in writing, what persuasive writing strategies you use to gain commitment and elicit co-operation, to point out to the receiver the features and benefits to him for his involvement, to commit to deadlines, and to ensure a quality product. What evolved from the session were some clear-cut strategies and techniques for getting through to your audience in memos, proposals and reports, and how to walk the human tightrope so that you are perceived as committed rather than pushy.

17 Persuasive Writing Strategies to Gain Commitment

A. Features and Benefits

1. Create an element of fun in your writing. Fun is a vital benefit humans cherish and constantly look for in everything they do and in the people they work with. This strategy will unwittingly engender commitment from the reader.
2. Highlight the features and benefits of the idea, service or product for the reader to get his attention and interest, build his desire to know more and to prompt him to act. AIDA (attention, interest, desire, action) is an old and effective marketing axiom.
3. Line up your power points. In a *Larson* comic strip, a gent just rising in the morning looks at a poster-size message taped to his wall: "First pants, then shoes." You persuade the reader when you line up your power points in the right order to clearly show the features and benefits to and for them.
    Remember! WIIFM — "What's in it for me?" says the reader.

B. "You" Focus

4. Use a personal tone rather than an impersonal one where appropriate. (For technical and scientific writing, use the impersonal.)
5. Concentrate on understanding the other person's point of view and in setting mutual goals. Don't judge, manipulate or control or sound arrogant.
6. Be caring and supportive of the reader's timeframes and schedule.
7. Compliment, congratulate, praise or acknowledge the other person's accomplishments or successes as appropriate.

8. Design your piece to appeal to and persuade the reader. Use combinations of headings, easy-to-read type, bold face, a mix of upper- and lower-case words, white space to break up text, spaces between lines and paragraphs, bullets, boxes and indents to highlight important points and graphics as appropriate.

   Remember! Labels are for jars and cans, but don't provide an all-encompassing description of "the whole reader" you are working with. Persuade by being accepting of people's differences.

C. Solidarity

9. Appeal to the reader's basic human needs for community and self-esteem (see Maslow, Chapter 7). Make the reader feel connected to the idea, service or product, and give him an opportunity to make a shining contribution.

10. Ask for help. Not assistance, commitment, co-operation or a contribution, but rather plain, old-fashioned "help." You'll be pleased with the warm response you will receive. Most people enjoy helping when and if they can.

11. Use the four magic words "I'd appreciate it if ..." This says so much more than "please" or "thank you."

12. Focus on expressions, jargon and acronyms the reader understands to form solidarity through language.

13. Find common ground and build on it to form solidarity through likemindedness.

14. Persuade through solidarity of expression. Remember to match, pace and lead your reader with a style and tone that he is comfortable with.

15. Explain to the reader why something is important to or for you. Speak to your commitment to the project and to meeting the deadline. Then let the reader know you appreciate his talent and skill in helping to make the project a reality. This sets up a scenario that says "you *and* me" rather than "you *or* me."

16. Make the first move to fix any kind of potential problem. This builds trust and respect, and will engender commitment. Go hard on the problem, easy on the reader.

17. Be sincere. Say what you feel and what you mean.

Remember! Stay clear of short-term negative motivators like guilt, threats, fear, intimidation or "you owe me" techniques. You win friends, build solidarity and gain commitment by helping people to feel good about themselves and about you.

Same Message, Multiple Audiences

Messages to multiple audiences require that people try to wade through messages that don't apply to them or are unnecessary. People can become angry if their time is wasted too often.

These messages can incur hostility when the receivers feel they are being manipulated. For example, people are sent blind copies on issues for the purpose of gaining exposure, covering their tracks, playing one-upmanship or gaining ground. Examples include:

> "She faxed our boss on this, too. I'm angry. If she had a problem with the way I'm handling this section of the project, *she should have come to me first.*"

> "He wouldn't listen to me, so I sent a memo to his boss in the States. He then got an answer from his boss and tagged on a *nasty message* and E-mailed it back to me."

Our Attitude

"Although aptitude and attitude are two separate entities, behaviour is produced through the interaction of both. A whole range of variables such as values, personality, beliefs, skills and knowledge impact this interaction."

- Marijane Terry, Partner, *Geller, Shedletsky & Weiss, Industrial Psychologists*

In *Man's Search for Meaning,* Viktor Frankl talks about our ability to choose our attitude regardless of the circumstances. Frankl believes the kind of person you become is the result of an inner decision, not external factors. Attitude cannot be measured. It is a matter of choice.[23]

But I Want To Speak To A Real Person!!!

Technology advocates abound. At the same time, there's still a contingency of reticent folks who have a good deal of fear and caution towards technology. David Morrison, vice president, human resource development, Toronto-Dominion Bank, makes the following observation: "Those of us that want real people to talk to are longing for a day in our past. The good old days when a chocolate bar was ten cents. Those days do not exist any more. Business has entirely different mediums today and they're here to stay. So people need to stop complaining about technology."

What Morrison and many of his contemporaries have found is that our attitude, or at least an inconsistent or fearful attitude toward technology, is paralysing a number of would-be technology users. Simply, technology is here to stay and we'd better get used to it, says Morrison. Adds Morrison, "The payoffs come for those who take the time to invest in learning to use the technology well. By practising."

Many organizations today are faced with management and staff who use technology not because they want to. In other words, technology has become a matter of compliance rather than commitment for many users.

Using and Choosing your Electronic Media

1. All the Time

Some people feel compelled to use technology all the time, even when meeting over coffee or lunch, or having a short person-to-person chat would be far more effective for certain situations and with certain individuals.

2. In Time

The all-the-time compulsion is also connected to our modern day "rush rush," make it happen, get it out and get it done way of doing business. Technology has increased our sense of immediacy to the point where some people feel compelled to react immediately. Points out Betty Vernassal, Senior Consultant with Forum Corp.: "If you can stop for a couple of seconds and think before reacting, it allows you to separate yourself from your work or your function. With technology we've come to answer instantaneously on E-mail and voice mail. I find that people expect this of themselves, and are uncomfortable in taking the time to think things through before they respond. Is faster always better? This is a trap we can all fall into easily if we allow it. The people we interact with deserve our consideration. So, take your time and think things through."

3. To Save Time

Some people use all types of technology interchangeably: there's no difference for them between a fax, an E-mail or voice mail. Their only goal is to reach the person as quickly as possible. They do not evaluate in advance the effectiveness of the particular medium for the quality of the message or its potential impact on the receiver.

People often gravitate toward the medium that is fastest for them to use. Often this precludes (a) the best medium for a particular type of communication, and (b) the receiver's preference. *Faster doesn't always mean better.* And in the end, it doesn't always save you time.

Choosing and Using Voice Mail, Fax and E-mail

As we examine all the factors that contribute to your decision in choosing a particular medium for your message, I'd like to briefly look at the ins and outs of using voice mail, faxing and E-mail.

Voice Mail Messages

1. What's appropriate?

- short, specific messages
- non-complicated, non-sensitive messages
- messages that are easily added to and shipped to a colleague

2. What's inappropriate?

- sensitive messages where one-on-one is needed by phone or with a person who "needs a human voice"
- complicated messages where dialogue is needed
- complicated messages where a visual is needed (budget analysis, spread sheet, thought piece, strategy piece)

3. Voice mail don'ts:

- promoting electronic wars
- badgering
- hiding
- creating invisible barriers — "the black hole syndrome"
- rambling
- venting

The Communications Survey

Many organizations are doing a variety of communication surveys to better understand how people want to send and receive messages. Lenscrafters International, a leading eyeglass manufacturer and retailer, completed a Canada-wide survey in February 1994 four months after voice mail was introduced. At that time, they discovered how unpopular voice mail was (only 1.6 percent of 511 surveyed said it was the most effective medium of communication for them). Since then, it has steadily gained in popularity.

Sue Carey, Group Operations Training Manager at Lenscrafters, believes the following: "We're a very hands-on, face-to-face organization. So it's taken a while for our people to see the benefits of voice mail. [As of May 1995, up to 50 percent were using voice mail regularly and saying it was effective.] But voice mail will never be a substitute for people. We do business face-to-face and that's how we relate to each other as people. [40.1 percent of 511 surveyed said meetings were the most effective method of communication for them.]

Voice Mail Communication Tips

1. Before you call, think about how you're feeling. Your tone of voice will affect how your message is interpreted and responded to. *Example:* Is your tone pleasant? anxious? enthusiastic? frustrated? Will your tone encourage or discourage a response by the listener? Will your tone create goodwill?

2. Phone messages need to be crisp: if the situation calls for more than a simple exchange of information, then ask the person to call you and leave a time(s) when you can be reached. *Example:* Hi, Ruth. It's Jerry Peel. I hope you're having a good day. Just wanted to let you know, Stan's got the figures you were looking for. He's around today after 10:00 at extension 613.

3. Give phone numbers slowly: it's an aggravating time waster to have to replay a message to catch the phone number.

4. Longer messages let people know up front (a) how important the message is, and (b) how long it is. If they're busy, or are not in the office and are calling in for messages, they can save the message and play it when they have more time. They will appreciate your thoughtfulness and consideration, and you will get a faster and more meaningful response.[24]

WE ARE "FULL OF PAPER": USING FAX AND E-MAIL

To frame our discussion for "wisely" using the fax and E-mail, let's turn our attention to written English for a moment. Despite all the fancy hardware, and the emphasis on oral and fast communication, we are still a society that's very full of paper. We use all sorts of formal and informal memos, letters, proposals and reports that come to us by mail, courier, fax, modem, E-mail and Internet. A colloquial E-mail may even imitate spoken language: "Wanna pop out for a bite on Friday?" But it's still written and can be printed off — and saved for time in memorium. Some previously formal customer service writing is now being replaced with shorter, friendlier, handwritten fax notes, but personal letters to customers plus all our internal correspondence still require that we write — and write well.

A client once told me about a situation where she gave one of her staff, a good writer, a proposal to review. On a sticky note she wrote, "Would you please go over this and we can chat about it at our meeting." Much to the client's surprise, she got back a lengthy, formal synopsis of the proposal. The client felt that too much time was spent on writing on or about things that could have been discussed verbally. But, in fact, the client had missed the point. The staffer took the assignment very seriously; by responding in writing he actually went the extra mile — he took the time to carefully frame his thoughts and to do a thorough job in giving her the feedback she needed.

Writing takes time, thought, creativity and energy. And when a person puts pen to paper, or fingers to keyboard, unless you know otherwise, work with the premise that he or she cares, and has made the time to share his or her thoughts and feelings. When a good friend is away and drops you a post card, how do you feel? Although telephones are now easy and affordable, building relationships in writing can be interesting and fun.

This is the same experience (and often hurt and disappointment arise) when people who are "writing sensitive" send personal notes (by mail or E-mail) — cards, postcards, letters, personal faxes —and children who make cards for family and friends, don't feel appreciated by the receiver. Following is Natalie's personal account of her friend Mitch's interpretation of a "welcome back card" she sent him. Intended for fun and to create solidarity in good news and common ground, the result was misinterpretation, lack of appreciation and lack of respect.

"I wanted to do something nice for Mitch to welcome him back from his photography shoot. On his last shoot, he'd wanted to capture a field of wildflowers but couldn't because of the weather. He was itching to get them this time, and told me so. So I hunted (and I mean hunted) for just the right card which had a lovely cascade of wildflowers on the front. Then I wrote in a fun message. When Mitch called me (three days after he'd been back) he said I sent him the card to manipulate him into calling me."

Writing Is Forever

In personal and professional relationships, writing can be seen as confrontational, intimidating or threatening as it was to Mitch. Here we see an example of our double bind again; too much solidarity can be a scary thing. And if there's a problem and it's set down in writing (as Jeremy did in Chapter 2, Potential Crash Site #7), things never have a chance to die out and go away. Unlike spoken speech, which is dynamic and flowing, written language is static, shaped, forever. Its static nature allows for reading and re-reading, for ongoing records, for the rehashing of good and bad news, and for chronicling. The reader can re-live the event and get angry all over again leaving little room to heal a touchy issue. So, before you write your message down, in a business situation or a personal one, carefully evaluate your options based on audience, purpose, content and situation.

The Writing Avoidance Syndrome

Following are two examples of what I call the "Writing Avoidance Syndrome." A common problem is using writing (fax, E-mail, inter-office mail, letter) to solve a problem that needs to be talked through so both sides are comfortable. In example #1, the writer avoided dealing with an issue and therefore, wrote. In example #2, frustrated, the writer wrote in an effort to generate a commitment where there was none.

EXAMPLE 1

Two colleagues and friends, Patty and Ian, have different expectations regarding a breakfast talk they are arranging to host together. Ian is totally frustrated and sends a fax to Patty, cancelling the project. Patty calls to speak with him; he's not in and she leaves a voice mail for him to return her call. Ian does not return the call. Patty is concerned and wants to solve the miscommunication, she goes to Ian's home later that day and leaves a note for him to contact her. She never hears from Ian. Patty is hurt and sad. She thinks she's lost a friend and a colleague.

ANALYSIS

When Patty and Ian finally do talk, Ian admits he didn't know how to handle the situation, so he avoided it by writing and sending Patty a fax. His intention (little did Patty know) was only to end the project because he was not comfortable with it. He did not intend it to be personal in any way. But Patty did take it personally because there was a friendship at stake (or so she thought). For Ian, the friendship was never in jeopardy. They quickly reconciled, and today their friendship is stronger than ever.

EXAMPLE 2

A manager speaks to his president and makes a number of productive recommendations which the president commits to giving him feedback on. A period of time passes and there is still no feedback as promised. The manager decides to recap their conversation in written form and informs the president that a draft is on it's way. Angry, the president demands to see a copy of the draft. When the president receives the draft, he puts it "on file" and never addresses the issues originally discussed.

ANALYSIS

The president paid "lip service" to the manager's recommendations and never had any intention of following through. When the manager called him on it in writing, he became defensive and ignored both the correspondence — and the original issues. Here, the manager may have had an impact face-to-face, but writing worked out to be a disadvantage.

I'd like to end this discussion on when to use writing on a very positive note, because I believe writing is one of the best ways to touch people. The written mode can be a powerful tool to get what you want and to build satisfying relationships along the way. A client once told me of a situation where he wrote regularly over a two-year period to a pensions clerk in England to obtain the retirement money he'd not received when he left that organization and moved to Canada. They built up a friendship and trust over the two years, and the clerk was able to get his funds released to him.

Written Messages (memo, fax letter, other)

1. What's appropriate?

– for quick, follow-up correspondence
– for short or long memos, proposals or reports where hard copy is wanted/needed
– for confirmations, notices, instructions
– to build relationships (ever had a pen pal?)

2. What's inappropriate?

– for avoiding a conversation where at minimum you need to connect with the other person and hear his voice to discuss an issue or solve a problem

Writing on Electronic Mail (E-mail)

The age of letter writing in the 1800s and 1900s, which many feel is a lost art form, is actually seeing its resurgence in modern day E-mail. People who are perhaps more reserved and business-like in the oral mode, are finding new ways to express themselves and enhance relationships on E-mail. Technology advocate David Morrison cites the following personal experience:

> "I had the opportunity to work closely with one of our senior vice-presidents on a pilot project. We had known each other for years and our relationship had always been cool and businesslike. We chose E-mail as the most effective way to communicate for the project based on our schedules and our project roles. Initially, our correspondence was formal but gradually more of our personalities began to show, humour was interjected, and an enhanced relationship was developed. Over the two to three months of the project, there were approximately 20 E-mail interchanges, and the nature of the relationship become much warmer and more friendly. This is now the case when we meet face-to-face."

Joseph Walther, a communications professor at Northwestern University in the U.S., has coined the word "hyperpersonal" to describe this phenomenon.[25] Not only does his research show that we are compelled to "really say what we think" on E-mail, but that this leads to making disagreements explicit and therefore better joint decisions among team members. Although hyperpersonal communication initially takes longer to forge social connections, the payoff is great. E-mail correspondence and work projects allow users to achieve more than they do face-to-face in terms of relationship building, consensus building and in high-quality group decision-making.

E-mail Messages

1. What's appropriate?

– quick follow up: clarification of dates, times
– for factual information such as lists, announcements, bulletins, to reach a wide audience with one push of the button

- short or longer messages (maximum three minutes of reading time)
- messages that need a visual (spreadsheet)

2. What's inappropriate?

- sensitive issues where one-on-one in person or by telephone may be needed
- for visual presentations and thought pieces where over three minutes of reading is required

3. E-mail don'ts:

- sending to everyone (including your mother)
- telling tongue-in-cheek jokes that could be misinterpreted (use icons such as smiley faces as needed if you are using humour)
- scapegoating

E-mail Communication Tips

➤ Ask yourself if this is the best medium to get your message across in and with this particular person. Will the reader feel comfortable receiving this message in writing? On the system? Who is the reader? What does he need to make a decision? Is a phone call needed? A face-to-face? A meeting? A lunch?

➤ If you decide to go with E-mail, then focus on: (a) giving a clear purpose, and (b) selecting content — the right kind, right amount. Example:

Benny: I'd appreciate your feedback on Monday's strategy session. Can we get together Friday at 11? Please confirm. Thanks. Edith.

Remember! You're writing for the other person, not for yourself.

➤ When dealing with a "hot topic," bang out your message and let it sit. Come back to the text for an objective edit before you fire off the final version. Your goal is to solve a problem, and this will be clear in the commitment you show in your message.

Remember! If you're skilled and ask the right questions, you'll get the information you need with either E-mail or voice mail.

Cut the Fat — Not the Food

For years I've heard complaints in organizations about not only when people write but how they write in memos, by fax and on E-mail. We have an added complication in writing: minus the verbal and body language, we are solely word dependent for both the content message and the relationship message. So good writers are sensitive to what they say and how they say it. To end this chapter, I want to briefly discuss what writing in fact "looks like" and leave you with a few tips on how to "cut the fat — not the food."

What Does Writing Look Like?

For example, when you read a novel, it is written to be read. And all the dialogue in a novel, just like the dialogues I've presented throughout this book, is written to be read as natural speech. In good speeches that you've heard, the speaker is working from a text written for the ear and not the eye. Think back to university, college or high school. Did you ever have a professor or teacher who lectured at you with a hard-to-understand written text that was written to be read, not to be spoken? This is a concrete example of what not to do. Make sure you write your message "right" so as to have a positive impact on the receiver. You want to turn them on and make your points — not frustrate them or put them to sleep.

Word Tips For Effective Written Messages

Following are some word tips that will come in handy for all your written communication.

1. Make Your Message Time Efficient

original: "objectives of the project"
word count: 4

rewrite: "project objectives"
word count: 2

Remember! Never say in four words what you can say in two.

2. Meet Your Audience's Needs

original: "A comprehensive assessment of the community needs and a careful selection of programs are critical to the ongoing success of the organization."

description: formal, impersonal, I focus
features and benefits: hidden
word count: 22

rewrite: "To ensure your ongoing success, we recommend a comprehensive community needs assessment followed by in-depth planning and selection."

description: formal, personal, You focus
features and benefits: up front
word count: 18

Remember! If it's appropriate, try and be personal. This will bring the reader into the text. As well, always use a "you focus." You're writing for someone else not yourself. By putting the features and benefits to the reader up front, you are certain to get and keep his attention.

3. Use Clear Language

original: "Thank you for the time you spent with me on Thursday discussing your information systems activities and sharing with us your aggressive expansion and franchising plans. As a result of that meeting, we are pleased to present our proposal to assist you in the acquisition and implementation of your next generation of information system to meet that revised need."

description: formal, personal, You focus, cumbersome, bulky nouns, info-dumps, gushy
word count: 59

rewrite: "I appreciate your taking the time on December 10, 1995 to meet and discuss your aggressive expansion and franchising plans. To meet your revised needs, I have developed a strategy to help you acquire and implement your next generation of information system."

description: formal, personal, You focus, clear and brief, active verbs, no info-dumps, sincere
word count: 42

Remember! Your goal is to always cut the saturated fats — long words get lean, nouns become verbs and get leaner. Try to stick to a maximum of 25 words per sentence. Skilled writers get and keep their readers' attention and build goodwill along the way.

So Strategy 9 of the *How Not To Take It Personally Action Plan* is to use technology well to enhance communication.

Let's review the four steps to increase our knowledge and apply them.

1. Recognize the factors that contribute to a person's comfort level (learning style, aptitude, judgement and common sense, attitude) in using certain technologies.
2. Evaluate why some messages are more appropriate in a specific medium and choose the "right" medium for your message.
3. Respond — don't react. This is easy to do because technology is so practical and increases the pressure and demands on us.
4. Use speaking and writing, respectively, to solve a problem and enhance a relationship — not create one.

Summary of Part III: Implement Your Communications Success Action Plan

In Chapters 7, 8 and 9, we built our communication skills, targeted challenging personalities to practise on and focused on technology to further enhance communication. In Chapter 10 we will discuss "gaining perspective" to make all our hard work stick.

PART IV

MAKE YOUR ACTION PLAN STICK

SUCCESSFUL COMMUNICATION REAPS REWARDS

"It's a funny thing about life. If you refuse to accept anything but the best, you very often get it."

- Somerset Maugham

Strategy 10: Practice and Build on Your Communication Success Habits

You knew when you started this book that there would be no magic cures for all the miscommunications that you've encountered in your lifetime.

Throughout *How Not To Take It Personally*, we've very quietly (and not so quietly) alluded to a very important fact: "human beings create their own hurts." *You are 100 percent in control* of how you choose to listen, interpret and respond to someone's comment or action, and whether or not you take something personally — even when the comment was intended that way. Therefore *you are 100 percent in control* of the success of every interaction.

Hurts and disappointments with people and in life are natural. But if you internalize these hurts, you'll just be compounding the disappointment by hurting yourself. What started as one problem will have mushroomed into two or more.

If *we*

L - Listen
I - Interpret
R - Respond
A - Appropriately!

we're most likely to accurately interpret the content message and the relationship message. But this isn't and can't always be the case. No one feels at his best all of the time. Everyone has bad days. We all feel defensive sometimes. We all whine — loudly, at least once in awhile. We simply aren't perfect. And whatever we are going through at the moment, and how we feel about our lives and ourselves impacts our interpretation of every situation. Humans truly are synergistic creatures. Like our bodies whose individual organs taken together produce a dynamic whole, so too do our minds reflect a myriad of individual differences. For this purpose, I would like to end this book in sharing my perspective on gaining perspective with you.

MY HELICOPTER VIEW OF LIFE

"Some people are so good at taking a professional, rather than an emotional, point of view. I remember working on a project that really panicked me. Everything was in a complete mess on my desk. I was in a state of total chaos. In her most professional tone, my boss, wiser than her years, an excellent manager who was remarkably perceptive, simply commented that what I was doing (i.e., surveying all my options) was a really effective way to begin. By objectively labelling my activity, she imposed structure on the situation and elevated me and the activity to her competent, very professional level."

> - Mary Anne Harnick, *Conference Director,*
> *The Canadian Institute, Toronto, Canada*

Several years ago I visited Iguazu Falls, the widest waterfall or *cataratas* in the world that intersect at the borders of Argentina, Brazil and Uruguay. On the Argentine side, I could walk right up to *La Garganta del Diabolo* (the Throat of the Devil). In the semi-tropical jungle, the spray from the falls enveloped me, and it was easy to get lost in the rush of the water, the spray, the sun, the bush, the heat. I was lost in the mist and clung to the dynamism of the moment.

When I took a helicopter ride over the falls on the Brazilian side, however, I gained a very different perspective of the falls. High up in the clouds, I had the whole picture, the whole vista: how big the world was, how the falls filled a significant (albeit small) chunk of that world, and how decidedly micro I was, as were all the other humans and creatures on earth.

Enroute back to Argentina by taxi, I gained yet another perspective. Having moved out of the sky and back toward the rush of the falls, I hit a midpoint: I'd seen the falls from both sides now. Now I understood the rush and the fury, and the unrelenting power of this natural cascading wonder.

And such is perspective. Standing in the rush of the falls, I could only have a micro view. I was completely absorbed in my interpretation of the moment. I was there — in the thick of it. Lost in the mist. But once in the helicopter, I could see another perspective and, indeed, the whole picture. In fact, I got a sense of the whole world and of life. Having experienced both, I was then able to come back to a halfway point, and learn to move back and forth. To walk the human tightrope. The result was a unified whole, a synthesis of big and small, of macro and micro. Of balance. This was one of the most powerful images of my life, and whenever I need to gain and regain perspective, I recall it.

WALKING THE HUMAN TIGHTROPE

Perspective, like all of the forms of learned behaviours we've discussed, develops on an ongoing basis and is dependent on how you choose to walk the human tightrope. There are people who curse the day and everything in it if it's raining outside. Perspective would help us to accept the rain if we thought about why it's so important. And we might feel even better if we were to consider the free carwash we were getting. Who likes to pay ten dollars for a carwash?

In a play titled *The Fever,* [26] the lead character, in conversation with the audience, tells us that we liked ice cream when we were kids. We all readily agreed! Then she asks us if being an adult meant we had to stop liking ice cream. Like the character in the play, I am always puzzled by the number of adults who think "giving up" is a necessary requirement for maturity. Growing older does not mean forgetting the things that made you happy and made you smile. This too is perspective.

I remember once coming home from a late movie with a friend. When we circled one of the levels in his underground, he nicked his door (he nicked in a whole side) against one of the walls. When we got out of the car, he examined the damage and said, "That's the *second time* I've done that," laughed, then added "Oh well, *it's not the end of the world*." And he was right. Perspective allowed him to place the incident productively, and helped him to move on. He co-owned the truck with his brother, and again perspective allowed him to wisely save the telling of the incident until the following morning. After all, why ruin his brother's evening, he concluded. There was nothing that could be done until the following morning, anyway. This, too, is perspective.

PERSPECTIVE MEANS LEARNING FROM YOUR MISTAKES

I remember once talking through an unpleasant situation with a renovations contractor whose van had just been vandalized. This man's process for dealing with problems was two-fold. First, he made a clear, conscious decision to see any situation including this one as "not a disaster." An excellent big picture framing strategy, he then asked himself a valuable small picture strategy: "What can I *learn* from this?" After I quietly attended his non-verbal answer (he was gaining perspective in his head), the practical coach in me asked if he had insurance. Guess what? He didn't!!! And the same vandals came back for round two to finish the job a week later (do you wonder why?), and there was still no insurance. So, what did he learn? Was he able to walk the human tightrope? Had he found the midpoint?

Canadian actor and singer Brent Carver (of *Kiss of the Spider Woman* fame)[27] believes that you've reached a point of balance within yourself when *you* question why you've made specific decisions and choices. I would add to this definition of balance, that you are comfortable with the answers you get from yourself. Because true balance for me means you understand yourself: how you think, behave, listen, speak and what motivates you to do what you do. The whole picture. Self-acceptance. The terrific, the good, the bad and perhaps the ugly. And in the words of my favourite diaper-bound philosopher, Trixie from the *Hi and Lois* comic strip: "It's good to be your own best friend." And I would add, no matter what.

Remember! There may be a couple of little bumps and not-so-little bumps along the yellow brick road. But when you find the wizard inside you, the balloon ride back to Kansas (or anywhere else you want to go) will be a worthwhile and meaningful adventure.

Lifetime Tips for Dealing with Goof-Ups

1. Deal with each new situation in isolation. Don't connect it to a past incident that caused you pain.

2. Detect the error. Look at the facts and the feelings.

3. Ask yourself what you learned.

4. Take that knowledge with you to the next business or life assignment. Your goal is to impact your performance using what you learned. In other words, apply your new-found knowledge and move forward.

5. Don't be angry with yourself. Sophocles said we're here to unravel the thread of life. Everyone comes into this life with a "full spool" (they come in different size spools of course) that gets unravelled and ravelled again. Remember, life's a spin.

6. Don't obsess. Get on with it. Life's awaiting.

7. Trust yourself not to repeat the same mistake.

8. Be prepared to make a new mistake — that's how you learn.

9. Peer Out the Front Window — Glance out the Back Window. In Bil Keane's *Family Circus* comic strip, an older sister is sharing her wisdom with her younger brother. She says that yesterday is the past and tomorrow is the future. But that today is a gift — that's why it's called the present.

10. What you resist, persists. Pay attention to your feelings and swim with the current.

The key premise behind *How Not To Take It Personally* is that to avoid taking things personally and to minimize hurt and disappointment, we need first to increase our self-awareness and self-knowledge. To do so, we've taken a journey that has enabled us to get better in touch with ourselves: how we think, how we listen, how we interpret, and how we respond. The following diagram wraps up the key concepts we have looked at in the book.

Remember! Make it Thy Business to Know Thyself. No one can do this for you.

Make It Thy Business To Know Thyself

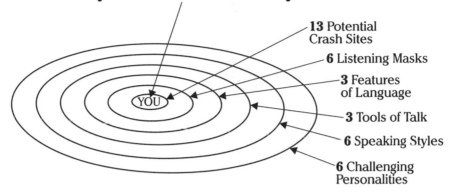

13 Potential
Crash Sites

6 Listening Masks

3 Features
of Language

3 Tools of Talk

6 Speaking Styles

6 Challenging
Personalities

CONCLUSION: GAINING PERSPECTIVE

"Man is ultimately self-determining ... every human being has the
freedom to change at any instant."

- Viktor Frankl

We create our own priorities and decide the degree of effort we
will put into these priorities. No one can do this for us. Something
is either important for you or it isn't, and the ongoing effort you put
into being a first-rate thinker and a top-notch communicator is up
to you. Equally, the quality of your results are up to you. So, if you
want quality thinking and quality communication in your personal
and professional life:

1. Understand who you are: your expectations, your perceptions,
   your listening masks, how you use the features and tools of language, your speaking style, your challenging personality.
2. Learn what your strengths are, and what areas you need to
   grow in.
3. Build successful communication habits based on these
   strengths and growth opportunities that constantly move you
   forward.
4. Create opportunities for continual growth.
5. Enjoy the ride (even the bumps).

And never, never, never take it personally!
(whether or not it was intended that way).

MEASURING YOUR PROGRESS

This book is designed to increase your self-awareness and self-knowledge as it relates to how you listen, interpret and respond, so let's re-do The Communication Skills Awareness Quiz and The Hurt Readiness Index that you completed at the end of Chapter 1 to determine how much you've grown.

The Communication Skills Awareness Quiz

Please circle your answers.

1. I set realistic expectations for myself.
   always   often   sometimes   rarely   never

2. I have realistic expectation of others.
   always   often   sometimes   rarely   never

3. My listening skills and habits are:
   excellent   very good   good   average   below average

4. Others think my listening skills and habits are:
   excellent   very good   good   average   below average

5. My interpretation skills and habits are:
   excellent   very good   good   average   below average

6. Others think my interpretation skills and habits are:
   excellent   very good   good   average   below average

7. My speaking skills and habits are:

    excellent   very good   good   average   below average

8. Others think my speaking skills and habits are:

    excellent   very good   good   average   below average

9. My all-round communication skills for dealing with challenging personalities are:

    excellent   very good   good   average   below average

10. Others think my all-round communication skills for dealing with challenging personalities are:

    excellent   very good   good   average   below average

11. My judgement skills for choosing the most appropriate medium (voice mail, fax, E-mail) for my message are:

    excellent   very good   good   average   below average

12. Others think my judgement skills for choosing the most appropriate medium (voice mail, fax, E-mail) for the message are:

    excellent   very good   good   average   below average

The Hurt Readiness Index

scale: 5 4 3 2 1 0

I would assess myself as:
5 - devastated by others' comments and actions
4 - frequently hurt and disappointed
3 - often hurt and disappointed
2 - sometimes hurt and disappointed
1 - rarely hurt and disappointed
0 - keep pin-pricks and bombs in perspective

14
ACTION
QUESTIONS

After reading this book and practising the strategies, techniques and steps I have learned, I can evaluate the following:

1. Am I more productive at work because I'm not spending time being hurt and disappointed?
2. Is my work better?
3. Can I finish a task faster?
4. Have my work relationships improved?
5. Do I feel confident to handle challenging personalities and difficult situations?
6. Have I risked new communication situations as a result of my increased confidence and performance? (list examples)
7. Am I feeling more satisfied with myself and my communication results?
8. Have I noticed the results of my enhanced thinking and communication skills? Be specific.
9. The three most useful things I have learned about myself in working with this book are...
10. The three behaviours that I have been able to change in myself working with this book are...
11. The three positive results in my performance that have come from my new behaviours are...

12. The three colleagues, boss, friend who can help me to keep practising my new thinking and communication behaviours are...

13. The three things that I am going to do to reinforce my new thinking and communication behaviours are...

14. The three people whose behaviour has been directly affected because there has been a change in my communication style are... How has their behaviour changed?

GIVING TO YOURSELF: THE KEY TO NOURISHMENT

In *First Things First,* Stephen Covey talks about committing "to the important" and in priority order. The most important commitment is to give to yourself, on a regular basis, and to nurture yourself emotionally, physically, spiritually and intellectually. So that's where we will start. If you acknowledge your true standards (not someone else's) you will achieve them. And if you fulfil your wants and needs on an ongoing basis, this self-knowledge and self-awareness will propel your communications growth.

Creating a Self-Nurturing Activity Chart

Create a chart listing how often you nurture yourself and are nurtured by others. Following is an example:

How Often You Get the Nurturing:

D - Daily
W - Weekly
M - Monthly
Q - Quarterly
S - Seasonally
A - Annually

Whether You Nurture Yourself or Receive It from Others:

I - I give it to myself

O - Others give it to me

The chart is divided into the four main nurturing areas: emotional, physical, spiritual and intellectual. As you can appreciate, categories may naturally overlap.

Following is an example of what a Self-Nurturing Chart might look like. Your goal in your chart is to have several "D's and W's" in column one and a balance of "I's and O's" in column two.

Remember! Self-approval, self-esteem and self-acceptance come from within.

The Self-Nurturing Activity Chart		
People/Activities	**How Often**	**I, O or Both**
1. Emotional		
my friends (especially Joe and Sally)	W	I and O
mother	W	I and O
wife	D	I and O
my pet	D	I and O
2. Physical		
my garden	W/S	I
curling club	W/S	I and O
squash	W (2 times)	I and O
treadmill	W (3 times)	I
3. Spiritual		
community theatre	W/S	I and O
fishing	W/S	I
committee work	M	I and O
music time with my child	W	I and O
4. Intellectual		
my clients	D	I and O
my colleagues	D-W	I and O
sales and marketing award	A	O
reading	D	I

Taking Credit

Do you take credit for your accomplishments? Ideally, the ratio that you are looking for is a balance between the strokes you give yourself, and the respect, love and appreciation you receive from others. If there are too many "O's" in the second column, you need to start trusting your own opinion and looking more to yourself for recognition and self-appreciation. Don't wait for pats on the back from others to feel good about yourself. Get the things you need to get done, done.

Self-Validation: Reinforce Your Own Successes

Whenever you've handled a communication situation well, and want to reinforce the successful habit, ask yourself:

1. Did I accomplish what I set out to do? (solve the problem, build the relationship, sell the idea)
2. Evaluate what steps you used to achieve your goals, and your comfort level with the process.
3. How can I accomplish more of the same?

Remember! You've got to trust your own opinion of your success, and not wait for pats on the back from others.

NOTES

1. I'd like to thank my friend Julie Michaels for sharing the music/dance metaphor with me, which I have developed.

2. I've built on Deborah Tannen's notion of "involvement and independence" which I have called community and autonomy (*That's Not What I Meant*, 1986, p. 31). The term "double bind" is originally Gregory Bateson's (1972) (Tannen, p. 33). I use "chronic double bind" to represent the constant push and pull of our competing needs for community and autonomy. Tannen's book is an inspiring resource for me and is recommended reading for anyone who wants to better understand the linguistic underpinnings of miscommunication.

3. I refer to power and solidarity throughout the book in terms of the balance or lack of it (our ability to walk the human tightrope) that is created in relationships due to the push and pull of competing needs. Key papers in this area are by R. Brown and A. Gilman, "Pronouns of Power and Solidarity," in T.A. Sebeok (ed.), *Style in Language*, (Cambridge, Mass.: MIT Press, 1960), pp. 253-76, and R. Brown and M. Ford, "Address in American English" in *Language and Culture and Society*, Pier Paolo Giglioli (ed.) (London: Penguin Books, 1972), pp. 252-282.

4. I attended a conference on the Learning Organization, June 21 and 22, 1993 where Hubert St. Onge, Vice President, Learning Organization and Leadership Development, Canadian Imperial Bank of Commerce, originally presented his concept of mindset. This discussion developed in a further conversation with the author.

5. I am using Deborah Tannen's (1986, p. 29) definition of "metamessage" which I call "relationship message" throughout the book. The original concept is from G. Bateson (1972).

6. This statistic is from Janis Foord Kirk's column "Career Monitor," *The Toronto Star*, 5 June 1993.

7. This discussion on the health benefits of listening is in J.J. Lynch, *The Language of the Heart: The Body's Response to Human Dialogue* (New York: Basic Books, 1985).

8. My ideas on monologue and dialogue come from two sources: theatre and language. I would like to thank my English professor, William Greaves, for first introducing me to these concepts (*The Language People Really Use,* Benson and Greaves, Book Society, 1973) in my first year at Glendon College, York University, which helped to shape my thinking of how people really talk to each other.

9. I am building on Michael Halliday's notion that spoken language is dynamic; see *Spoken and Written Language* (London: Oxford University Press, 1985).

10. For further information on the classic Sapir-Whorf Hypothesis, see Benjamin Whorf, (1956) "Science and Linguistics," in *Language, Thought and Reality: Selected Writings of Benjamin Lee Whorf,* Jon B. Carroll (ed.) (Cambridge, Mass.: MIT Press).

11. This discussion has been adapted from Robert Kaplan's discussion of paragraph structure in various languages in his 1966 article "Cultural Thought Patterns in Intercultural Education" in Kenneth Croft, ed. *Readings on English as a Second Language* (Cambridge, Mass.: Winthrop, 1972) p. 257.

12. This discussion of English breakdowns has been adapted from R.E. McConnell, *Our Own Voice* (Toronto: Gage Educational Publishing, 1979) p. 10.

13. I am building on linguist Noam Chomsky's theory of competence and performance (1965) and I am tying these ideas to what I am calling "style gaps" that arise from language and speaking style differences.

14. I am grateful to Deborah Tannen (1986) for her discussion on the signals and devices of conversational style (pp. 45-87) which, in conjunction with other linguists, has helped me over the years to shape my thinking in this area. For further reading in this area see John Gumperz, *Discourse Strategies* (Cambridge: Cambridge University Press, 1982) and the bibliography in this book.

15. This is Tannen's example of conversation management (1986, p. 182) which I am calling "topping."

16. I am grateful to a number of theorists who have researched and written in the areas of thinking and psychology, linguistics, communication style and character development, and who have influenced the design of the Six Speaking Styles. These are Sigmund Freud, Eric Berne, Carl Jung, Carl Rogers, Katherine Briggs, Isabel Briggs Myers,

Constantin Stanislavski, Deborah Tannen and Linda McCallister. Plus all the various communication style models I've been exposed to over the years in Neurolinguistics, Personality and Social Style, Trainer, Learner and Consulting Styles. Linda McCallister's book, *"I Wish I'd Said That"* (New York: John Wiley & Sons, 1992) is a wonderful resource and is recommended reading for anyone who wishes to pursue the area of 360 feedback and communication competencies, and would be interested in her Communication Style Profile.

17. I'd like to thank my business acquaintance Elaine Dembe for her expression "I am enough" at her June 13, 1995 presentation in Toronto.

18. The movie *Forrest Gump* was produced by Paramount Pictures, 1994.

19. The microscope and slide technique is Dr. Judith Segal's in her book *Dealing with Difficult Men* (New York: HarperCollins, 1994).

20. The expression "water seeks its own level" is from Dr. Laura Schlessinger's *Ten Stupid Things Women Do to Mess Up Their Lives* (New York: Villard Books, 1994).

21. The movie *The Princess Bride,* starring Billy Crystal, was produced by Twentieth Century Fox Corporation, 1987.

22. I am adapting Halliday's notion (1985, p. 97) that spoken language is active and that written English "exists"; communication isn't identical in the two modes.

23. Attitude choice is a constant theme of Viktor Frankl's in *Man's Search for Meaning* (New York: Washington Square Press, 1959).

24. The tip on leaving "considerate" longer voice-mail messages is from my friend Paul Litwack, Leadership Consultant, Litwack & Associates, Toronto.

25. Joseph Walther's notion of hyperpersonal is presented in Karin Vergoth's article, "Let's Get Hyperpersonal" in *Psychology Today* (July/August 1995).

26. *The Fever,* by American playwright Wallace Shawn, was produced in the winter of 1992 at Toronto's Tarragon Theatre with Clare Coulter as the lead character.

27. This is a paraphrasing of Brent Carver's view on balance in Vit Wagner's article "Balancing Act," *The Toronto Star,* 23 July 1995. *Kiss of the Spiderwoman,* starring Brent Carver, is the 1992 Tony Award winning musical produced by The Live Entertainment Corporation at the St. Lawrence Centre for the Arts, Toronto.

BIBLIOGRAPHY AND SUGGESTED READINGS

Bateson, Gregory. *Steps to an Ecology of Mind.* New York: Ballantine Books, 1972.

Benson, James, and Greaves, William. *The Language People Really Use.* Toronto: The Book Society of Canada Limited, 1973.

Berne, Eric. *Games People Play.* New York: Ballantine Books, 1964.

Booher, Dianna. *Communicate with Confidence.* New York: McGraw-Hill Inc., 1994.

Brown, H.D. *Principles of Language Learning and Teaching.* New Jersey: Prentice-Hall Inc., 1980.

Brown, R., and Gilman, A. "The Pronouns of Power and Solidarity." (1960) In *Style in Language*, edited by Thomas Sebeok, 253-276. Cambridge, Mass.: The MIT Press.

Brown, R., and Ford, M. "Address in American English." In *Language in Culture and Society,* edited by D. Hymes, 234-244. New York: Harper and Row, 1964.

Buscaglia, Leo. *Living, Loving & Learning.* New York: Ballantine Books, 1982.

Campbell, J. (ed.) *The Portable Jung.* New York: Penguin Books, 1991.

Chomsky, Noam. *Aspects of the Theory of Syntax.* Cambridge., Mass: The MIT Press, 1965.

Chomsky, Noam. *Language and Mind.* New York: Harcourt Brace Jovanovich, 1972.

Coloroso, Barbara. *Kids are worth it!* Toronto: Somerville House, 1995.

Covey, Stephen. *The 7 Habits of Highly Effective People.* New York: Simon & Schuster, 1989.

Covey, S., Merrill, A.R., and Merrill, R. *First Things First.* New York: Simon & Schuster, 1994.

Croft, Kenneth, ed. *Readings on English as a Second Language* Cambridge, Mass.: Winthrop, 1972.

Ervin-Tripp, S. "Sociolinguistic Rules of Address" (1969). In *Sociolinguistics,* edited by Pride and Holmes, 225-240. London: Penguin Books, 1972.

Fisher, Roger, and Ury, William. *Getting to Yes.* New York: Penguin Books, 1983.

Ford Kirk, J. "Career Monitor." *The Toronto Star,* 5 June 1993.

Forward, Susan. *Toxic Parents.* New York: Bantam Books, 1989.

Frankl, Viktor. *Man's Search For Meaning.* New York: Washington Square Press, 1959.

Freeman, A., and DeWolf, R. *The 10 Dumbest Mistakes Smart People Make and How to Avoid Them.* New York: HarperCollins, 1992.

Fulghum, Robert. *All I Really Need to Know I Learned in Kindergarten.* New York: Ivy Books, 1986.

Haden Elgin, Suzette. *Genderspeak.* New York: John Wiley & Sons, 1993.

Haden Elgin, Suzette. *BusinessSpeak.* New York: McGraw-Hill Inc., 1995.

Hall, Edward. *The Hidden Dimension.* New York: Doubleday & Co., 1966.

Halliday, Michael. *Spoken and Written Language.* London: Oxford University Press, 1989.

Held, V. "Banking on Words." In *Canadian Banker Magazine* (March/April 1993).

_____. "Keys to Making Winning Connections." In *Canadian Management Association Magazine* (October 1993).

_____. "People and Technology — Establishing a Comfort Zone." In *Canadian Banker Magazine* (September/October 1994).

_____. "Hiring Customer Service People: What to Look For." In *Hiring and Firing Magazine* (March 1995).

Hertzler, J.O. *A Sociology of Language.* New York: Random House, 1965.

Jespersen, O. *Language, Its Nature, Development and Origin.* New York: W.W. Norton & Co., 1964.

Killinger, Barbara. *The Balancing Act.* Toronto: Key Porter Books, 1995.

Lynch, James. *The Language of the Heart: The Body's Response to Human Dialogue,* New York: Basic Books, Inc., Publishers, 1985.

Maltz, Maxwell. *Psycho-Cybernetics.* New York: Pocket Books, 1969.

Maslow, A. H. *Toward a Psychology of Being* (2d ed.). Princeton, N.J.: Van Nostrand, 1968.

McCallister, Linda. *"I Wish I'd Said That!"* New York: John Wiley & Sons, 1992.

McConnell, R.E. *Our Own Voice*. Toronto: Gage Education Publishing, 1979.

Mehrabian, A. *Nonverbal Communication*. New York: Addline-Atherton, 1972.

Myers, Isabel Briggs. *Gifts Differing*. California: Consulting Psychologists Press Inc., 1980.

Ralston, Faith. *Hidden Dynamics*. New York: American Management Association, 1995.

Schlessinger, Laura. *Ten Stupid Things Women Do to Mess Up Their Lives.* New York: Villard Books, 1994.

Segal, Judith. *Dealing With Difficult Men.* New York: HarperCollins, 1994.

Tannen, Deborah. *That's Not What I Meant! How Conversational Style Makes or Breaks Your Relations with Others.* New York: Ballantine Books, 1986.

Vergoth, Karin. "Let's Get Hyperpersonal." In *Psychology Today,* (July/August 1995).

Wagner, Vit. "Balancing Act." *The Toronto Star.* Entertainment Section, p. B5, 23 July 1995.

Whorf, Benjamin. "Science and Linguistics" (1956). In *Language, Thought and Reality: Selected Writings of Benjamin Lee Whorf* edited by John B. Carroll. Cambridge, Mass.: MIT Press.

ABOUT
THE
AUTHOR

Vera N. Held, M.Ed., is a communications coach, speaker and writer and runs VNH Communications based in Toronto, Canada. She holds undergraduate degrees and certificates in English, Public Relations and Teaching English as a Second Language, as well as a Master's Degree in Education. She is a consultant and facilitator in the division of Executive Development at Toronto's York University and is on the faculty of The Institute of Advanced Technology in Toronto. She has worked with the Chiyoda Chemical Company and the Nippon Electric Company in Tokyo, Japan and in Canada with Vickers & Benson Advertising, The Equion Group, Glaxo Canada, Bell Canada, Hitachi Construction, Bombardier, Reuter's Canada, The Toronto Dominion Bank and others.

Some of Vera's interests and hobbies include her plant, pierrot and flower pot collections, modern Canadian theatre, watercolours, writing poetry, speed walking, international travel, Andean and 1960s music, antique jewellery, Hot Air Ballooning, reading to her friends' children, and her beautiful Abyssinian cat "Abbey," who is very happy the book is finished. Vera lives in Toronto, Canada and *How Not To Take It Personally* is her first book.

FOR MORE INFORMATION

For more information about consulting and coaching services, workshops and speaking topics, please contact:

Vera N. Held
VNH Communications
P.O. Box 85503
875 Eglinton Ave. West
Toronto, Ontario, Canada
M6C 4A8

Consulting, Coaching, Workshops and Speeches include:
1. How Not To Take It Personally
2. How to Create Realistic Expectations for Yourself and Others
3. Making Winning Connections: How to Create and Build Rapport
4. Listening Inclined: How to Get and Give Feedback
5. How to Create a Guide to Your Listening and Speaking Styles
6. How to Deal with Challenging Personalities
7. Understanding the Change Process
8. Making Winning Presentations
9. How to Write with Power and Impact
10. Using Technology to Enhance Your Communication
11. How to Understand People from Other Tongues and Lands
12. Executive-Sounding Board Program

Index